A. S. Migs Damiani

# CREATIVE LEADERSHIP
## Mining the *GOLD* in Your Workforce

*With a Foreword by Zig Ziglar*

S$^t$L

St. Lucie Press
Boca Raton   Boston   London   New York   Washington, D.C.

Excerpts from *The Speaker's Sourcebook* by Glenn Van Eckeren, copyright 1988. Reprinted with permission of Prentice Hall. Excerpt from *New Work Habits for a Radically Changing World* by Price Pritchett, Ph.D., copyright 1994 with permission from Pritchett and Associates. Other excerpts courtesy of Zig Ziglar, Ziglar Training Systems; Rich "MR POS" Wilkins, POS Publications; Ragan Communications, *The Working Communicator*; Brian Tracy, Nightingale Conant Corp.; Jay Kenney, Ph.D.; John Houghton; Dr. William R. Allen; Dr. Robert Rosen, Healthy Companies Group; and Francie Dalton, Dalton Alliances.

**Library of Congress Cataloging-in-Publication Data**

Damiani, A.S. Migs
    Creative leadership: mining the gold in your workforce / A.S. Migs Damiani
        p.  cm.
    Includes bibliographical references.
    ISBN 1-57444-226-0
    1. Leadership.   2. Creative ability in business.  I. Damiani, A.S. Migs.  II. Title.
HD57.7.D35    1998
658.4'092—dc21                                        98-4451
                                                  CIP

This book is dedicated to

**Christine Lynn Reid**

February 2, 1965 – December 23, 1996

who, while on this earth, did the best she could using the abilities that she had. Despite her handicaps, Christine achieved her goal to be self-sufficient and become a contributing member of society.

# Contents

# About the Author

 A.S. Migs Damiani is President of The Donohoe Companies' Mechanical Systems Operations Division, commercially known as Complete Building Services (CBS), which maintains over 13 million square feet of space in the Washington metropolitan area. CBS is a leading provider of facilities operation and maintenance services including design review, facility inspections/audits, energy conservation programs, CMMS programs, IAQ, installation, repairs and maintenance, and operation and management of many different types of facilities.

Prior to joining CBS in 1994, Migs was the Director of the Department of Facilities and Services for Montgomery County, Maryland. His department provided real estate, design and construction, maintenance and a myriad of services to all agencies (excluding schools) of the Montgomery County Government, involving over 190 buildings. Migs was formerly President of COM•SITE International, a firm specializing in data center planning, construction and maintenance; Director of Corporate Facilities/Administrative Services for Planning Research Corporation; and Manager, Corporate Facilities for Fairchild Industries. He has spent over 30 years as a corporate facilities executive, serving as president or reporting directly to Board Chairs and Company Presidents. As the Owner Representative, he has been responsible for the design, development, and maintenance of over 125 major building projects.

Migs holds a B.S. degree in Commerce and Engineering from Drexel University and a M.S. in Engineering Administration from The George Washington University. He has been named Plant Engineer of the Year by The American Institute of Plant Engineers (AIPE), recently renamed The Association for Facilities Engineering (AFE), and is a Fellow of AIPE and an Honorary Life Member of the American Institute of Architects (AIA). Migs is the author of *Looking for the Gold*, a values-based book that focuses on Total Quality in facilities management; *"Creative Leadership: Mining The Gold in Your Workforce"*; over 60 technical articles; six cover features; and chapters in two hi-tech real estate books.

Mr. Damiani is a graduate of The Center For Creative Leadership and has been a guest lecturer at The George Mason University, Georgetown University, The University of Maryland, Penn State University, and James Madison University. He has received over 30 national awards in his distinguished career and is a frequent speaker at national engineering and maintenance conferences. Migs also conducts specialized "people skills" training for industry, government agencies, colleges and universities, hospitals, and professional societies.

# Advance Praise

"For every manager who aspires to lead, for every first line supervisor who aspires to the next level of leadership, and for every individual who aspires to significantly change the world, Migs has collected an inspiring manual of leadership tools and techniques!"

—Fran Craig, President, *Computer Strategies*

"The most important asset of companies will be their intellectual capital. The keys to cultivating the human intellect are addressed in *Creative Leadership*. The book is about leadership skills needed to nurture personal and professional growth among employees and others."

—Dr. Finna Bjarnadottir, President, *LEAD Consulting*

"*Creative Leadership* is a book that explains, among other things, the difference between managing (things) and leading (people). Anyone who is responsible for the productivity of other people and who doesn't know the difference between managing and leading can learn many important lessons from this book."

—Larry K. Beck, Editor-in-Chief, *Engineer's Digest*

"I've always been puzzled over how few of our leaders know how and what can be done to involve and motivate employees. This is probably why we have so many managers and so few true leaders. *Creative Leadership* addresses these issues very well and should be read by anyone in a leadership position today or hopeful of being a leader in the future."

—Michael Kelly, Vice President, Corporate Real Estate, *PRC Inc.*

"Wherever you are in your journey through the densely populated forest of leadership aids, this book is the next step. Every page whittles a bit more of the bark from the boughs of seasoned, mature leadership, revealing a system of leading others that is strongly rooted in the rough and tumble realism of day to day business. Follow along as Migs helps you spawn new growth in others, and gives you all the tools you'll need to nurture, prune and strengthen the leaders of tomorrow who are reporting to you today."

—Francie Dalton, President, *Dalton Alliances*

"Migs has injected his personal knowledge of people skills into his writing in a way that can be easily understood and implemented. This "how-to" book is a winner. I'm impressed!"

—Robert Hummer, President, *Association for Facilities Engineering (AFE)*

"During his distinguished career, Migs Damiani has *positively* affected thousands of peoples' lives and careers. In his new book *Creative Leadership*, he shares his success formula with you to build more effective leaders - by looking for and mining the gold in your workforce - and to develop your people skills."

—Rich "MR POS" Wilkins, Author, Speaker, Motivator

"We live in an age of unforgiving management responsibility."

— *Creative Leadership*

"Managers owe it to their associates and themselves to move beyond the management of things to the leadership of people. This book is a terrific step forward toward that goal.

Migs has flavored the broth of his own extensive experience with Bill Bennett's *Book of Virtues*, Canfield and Hansen's *Chicken Soup for the Soul*, Covey's *Principle-Centered Leadership*, and a heavy portion of Zig Ziglar's *See You at the Top*."

—Larry Cain, Vice President, *Boland Services*

"Migs Damiani not only talks the talk, he walks the talk. Everything you'll read in this book represents Migs' style of leadership and provides us with a model that will serve us well if we are to be successful in the twenty-first century."

—Ron Nestor, Regional Manager of Human Resources,
*Bechtel Group (Retired)*

"*Creative Leadership* takes complex issues and provides simple, practical steps in creating an environment that is both rich and exciting for the employee as well as the company. The success stories that are included show how the principles and steps that are detailed work in actual situations. Migs has written a book that is not only extremely informative, but is both enjoyable and inspirational. His book clearly show that leaders are not limited to the management staff, but can be *any* member of the organization."

—Judy Stein, Consultant, *Radix® Solutions*

# Foreword

Migs Damiani has come up with a winner. *Creative Leadership —
Mining the Gold In Your Workforce* is a book written for this time
by a man who's "been there and done that". Migs has the capacity,
background, and success to deal with each phase of this subject in
an intriguing and challenging way. He touches all the bases and his
examples, illustrations, and procedures are solid. He uses a system
of teaching and inspiring which is thousands of years old and has
been used by the greatest teachers of all time, including the carpen-
ter from Galilee. Migs Damiani takes old-fashioned principles, give
them a modern twist, and applies them in a specific way that will
make each leader more effective not only in the market place but
in their personal and family lives as well.

   *Creative Leadership* gives specific, clear-cut directions not
just for those who are in leadership positions, but those who want
to be more, do more and have more. His integrity comes through
loudly and clearly as he repeatedly gives credit to the sources
which he quotes. He ties it all together in an interesting and
informative way, and hits major points with bullet-like precision,
effectively using "nuggets" of information that you can use in your
personal, family, and business life.

   Here is a book you can open to almost any page and get useful
information. You can spend a few minutes reading a chapter and
get some profound thinking and solid advice. You can take the
entire book, which I encourage you to do, and have a game plan
for getting more of the things money will buy and all of the things
money won't buy. Although he doesn't specifically mention either

of these things, this book will tell you how to get them both. I encourage you to read it thoroughly and carefully; then keep it handy as a reference. The principles have been around for a long time and they're going to survive indefinitely.

Zig Ziglar, *Over The Top*

# Preface

*"I will pay more for the ability to deal with people than any other ability under the sun."*

John D. Rockefeller

Prior to writing this book, I looked back at my own career to determine what was important in getting to the top. Fundamental values such as honesty, integrity and character came to mind, along with desire, hard work, and faith. These traits are characteristic in all successful leaders. I believe that the real "difference-makers" and most important qualities of success (and most difficult to master) are having and maintaining a positive attitude, the ability to work with and motivate people, possessing communications skills, and having goals. This is what leadership is all about.

*Creative Leadership* presents these crucial elements of success and will motivate you to use them daily in order to reinforce/develop your leadership skills. Leadership is an attitude before it becomes an ability or skill, and people are at the heart of it all. People are the most important, and often the most forgotten, ingredient in a company. They are also the greatest untapped natural resource and the most expensive in any organization. According to Brian Tracy, only five percent of employees feel that they are producing at full capacity. Involving people and motivating them by example is a trait found in all successful leaders, and in my book you will learn how to motivate and energize employees through creative leadership.

I have written this book for aspiring leaders and managers who want to acquire new skills, become flexible, and re-engineer themselves in order to thrive in our fast-changing world. I have used my real-life experience and specialized training as a graduate of The Center for Creative Leadership and facilitator of Zig Ziglar's "See You At The Top" and "Strategies for Success" programs in developing this leadership manual. Helping you reach your full potential as a leader is one of the goals of my book.

Many management resources and periodicals indicate that CEOs across the country are united on mentors and mentoring. Not only do they have mentors themselves, they mentor many others. That has been the case with me and I have dedicated a chapter to the subject. The key to successful employee development is communicating vision and values, then seeing that the employee lives the vision and exemplifies the values. Loyalty is welded in place by mentors who share their company's philosophy with others on a daily basis.

Mid- and senior-level managers whose styles have been dictatorial, explosive, non-decisive, uncommunicative, lethargic, and politically motivated need to revamp their work style. Today's environment requires us to accept and lead change and accept less security as facts of life. Doing so requires leaders to be more communicative and more trusting of employees. You will learn how to create positive, caring workplaces and to encourage employees to become the best they can be. And, you will learn how to cope with and lead change in the process.

It is also important to understand your employees' wants and fears — I believe this book will help show you how to meet employees' needs and overcome their fears. People need to feel important. How you can make others around you feel important and successful is a great difference maker. The only thing that you have that your competition does not is *your* employees. When they feel good about themselves, they will do better work and be more productive. The simplest yet most powerful tenet of leadership — a critically important yet most frequently overlooked truth — is how important it is to make others feel important. When you do, you will be important.

Learning how to appraise your management style and that of others, and then to work well with others is another important skill to acquire. You will learn how to look for the right "yes" rather than always saying "no," to cultivate a winning team identity and spirit, and to influence others to lead. At one time I thought that only extroverts had the makings of leaders, but experience has taught me that is not true. Leadership consists of the ability to create a vision, to communicate it, and to mobilize people to carry it out. Extroverts may excel at person-to-person communication, especially in mobilizing people, and building excitement, but vision creation is a natural for the introvert. Introverts tend to lead through technical know-how and others follow them because of their expertise. Everyone needs to acknowledge his or her shortcomings and to make a commitment to improve those skills. Today's leadership challenges require all of us to be interdependent and work well with others. The more we know about ourselves, the better we can understand the dynamics of personality.

Over the years, I have determined that the topics included in this book are those that made the greatest impact on my own success and they can do the same for you. I have also learned that having and maintaining a positive attitude is fundamental to success. Nothing constructive can be accomplished with a negative attitude. I have designed this book as an easy-to-use resource you will want to refer to time and again for reinforcement. Use it as such, and you will not only find reinforcement for yourself, you will also be prepared to "find the gold in others."

## A Good Leader

A good leader job requires certain skills,
That not many people are able to fulfill.

A good leader mustn't cave under pressure,
And must possess inside strength of infinity measure.

A good leader must see and look beyond,
And not flaunt when he's right, but admit when he's
wrong.

A good leader must be gentle and wise,
He must be honest, and tell no lies.

A good leader must be patient, loyal, and kind,
He must keep an open state of mind.

A good leader is filled with imagination,
He must enjoy his occupation.

A good leader must be trusting and bold,
He must be warm, and never cold.

Now that you know what a good leader needs,
Will you follow, or will you lead?

by Rachel Houghton, age 13

## Effective Leadership

To increase leadership effectiveness, managers should:

- Be flexible, not rigid. Recognize that there is no one best way to lead.
- Avoid being preoccupied with control. Monitor performance in terms of results relative to goals.
- Use a persuasive personality to get things done. Avoid the force of power unless absolutely necessary.
- Balance an emphasis on getting the job done with a concern for personal feelings and relationships.
- Do whatever it takes to help the group attain its goals.
- Keep channels of communication open. Be available. Maintain an effective flow of two-way communication.
- Set the pace for the group by being a positive example. Be enthusiastic and action-oriented. Set high standards.
- Represent followers effectively both laterally and upward in their organization. Have individuals who originate unique ideas or do outstanding work make the presentation of these ideas and work to higher management.
- Serve as a buffer to protect followers from pressure, uncertainty, and frustration.
- Do whatever it takes to help followers become the best they can be. Make a special effort to help followers who are deficient in any aspect of their jobs.
- Match individuals to jobs that suit them.
- Work to empower followers. Give followers opportunities to show their capabilities and grow professionally. Help followers prepare themselves for jobs to which they aspire.
- Provide deserved performance feedback, both positive and negative, using public praise and private criticism. Provide recognition and rewards that are commensurate with performance.

- Define the leader role as being separate and distinct from that of followers. Avoid being either too close or too distant. Avoid striving to be the best-liked member of the group.
- Involve followers in plans, goals, decisions and processes that affect them.
- Make a genuine effort to understand followers. Know their strengths and weaknesses, personal goals, and career interests. Be sensitive to factors causing follower dissatisfaction. Resolve conflicts in a timely manner. Be a good listener.

— William R. Allen, Ph.D.
William R. Allen Associates, Narragansett, RI

# Acknowledgments

I am blessed with many great teachers and associates who have graced my life and taught me many things that have made me a better person.

First and foremost is my wife, Helen, who has been my life partner and best friend in family and personal matters. I don't know what I would do without her. Thank you Helen, for being a terrific wife and caring mom and grandmother.Then, there are Lisa and David, my children and my grandchildren — Ryan, Kerry, and Kim. I am so proud of all of you! Thank you for the joy you bring to me.

To my many friends who bring out the best in me and especially. Jack and Jean Reid, and their children — Christine, Buck and Julie. I have dedicated this book to Christine, who passed away last year.

To all my mentors who are mentioned in the book and others who, through ignorance, I failed to mention. A special thanks to Zig Ziglar for encouraging me to write two books and being a role model, par excellence.

With all my heart I wish my mother were here to share this accomplishment with me. The strong foundation she gave me indelibly shaped my view of right and wrong and my sense of personal responsibility.

I am blessed to be associated with Dudley Kay, President and founder of SciTech Publishing. As my agent and broker, he took my ideas, offered great counsel, and helped me to produce a book of which I am very proud.

I would also like to express my gratitude to my publisher at St. Lucie Press, Acquisitions Editor Drew Gierman, who strongly recommended that this book be published. And to the St. Lucie production staff — Carolyn Spence, Carolyn Lea, Helen Linna, Connie Grigutis, Denise Craig, and Vicki Mitchell — it was a joy working with such professionals.

Thanks also to John Dermatas and Cindy Smith for helping me personally in getting my manuscript in the proper format and teaching me more computer skills than I thought possible.

To all my associates and fellow employees — both past and present — my sincere thanks to you. Without you, none of this would have been possible and I am deeply grateful for your help, understanding, and inspiration. Thank you for giving me so much.

# Introduction

*"You can dream, create, design and build the most wonderful place in the world...but it requires people to make the dream a reality."*

Walt Disney

In order to claim a leadership role in the global economy, American business needs more and better leaders — business professionals who are committed to their communities, their industries, and their companies as they are to their own careers. We need young men and women with a clear sense of values, integrity, and professional protocol who can communicate effectively, problem-solve creatively, and have top-notch technical and people skills.

*Creative Leadership* is written for leaders and aspiring leaders who are committed to continual improvement and the development of solutions to the challenges of an ever-increasing competitive market.

Corporations are looking for leaders instead of managers, i.e., people who are going to create rather than manage assets, people who can make the difficult decisions while recognizing others' feelings, people who can make a difference. Making the necessary changes — shifting from a cost-cutting to a values-creation orientation, from command-and-control to *trust* — is not easy.

*Creative Leadership* will show you how to develop or reinforce influential "people skills" that you can immediately put to use to achieve greater success as a leader — and more quickly. It will also help you develop a positive, caring workplace, which is needed to motivate and energize your workforce.

Learn how to lead by example, develop a positive attitude, make others feel important, manage confrontation, lead change, communicate with others, motivate yourself and others, mentor employees, and develop/reinforce your leadership potential. You'll find the concepts in this book easy to read, simple to understand, and very effective to use. Inspirational sayings and success stories are included to boost your confidence and to give you courage.

Succeeding as a leader in the 21st century will require continual learning, especially in the area of "people skills." We will need to pay more attention to what's important to others and not write-off uncooperative people.

Use of influence will become a common buzz word in leadership training. Effective influence begins with an awareness (a very deep listening to ourselves) of the way we think and believe and value those we want to influence. Influence is gained by engaging in mutually beneficial exchanges.

Learning about ourselves and others will become another skill that will make a difference to aspiring leaders, and applying what we learn will be the real difference in determining whether or not we'll be successful. Hopefully, what you read and learn in this book will prepare you well to survive and thrive in the 21st century.

At the end of each chapter, several Success Stories are included which, hopefully will inspire you to implement the material and recommendations contained in the chapter. Many of the stories are from *The Speaker's Sourcebook* by Glenn Van Ekeren.

# SUCCESS STORIES

## It's An Uphill Climb

As Paul Harvey once said, "You can tell when you are on the road to success. It's uphill all the way."

A young man in Kansas City, with a burning desire to draw, understood the uphill climb to success. He went from newspaper to newspaper trying to sell his cartoons. But each editor coldly and quickly suggested that he had no talent and implied that he might want to choose another line of work. But he persevered, determined to make his dream a reality. He wanted to draw, and draw he would.

For several months, the rejections came. Finally, in a move of "grace," he was hired by a minister to draw pictures advertising church events. This young artist was not discouraged by his unusual opportunity. Rather, he remembered the wise words of Benjamin Disraeli: "The secret of success in life is for a man to be ready for his opportunity when it comes."

Working out of a small, mouse-infested shed owned by the church, he struggled to be creative. Ironically, this less-than-ideal working environment stimulated his most famous work. He called it Mickey Mouse. And, of course, the man of whom we are talking was Walt Disney.

*- The Speaker's Sourcebook*

## Children Learn What They Live

If a child lives with criticism
he learns to condemn.

If a child lives with hostility
he learns to fight.

If a child lives with ridicule
he learns to be shy.

If a child lives with shame
he learns to feel guilty.

If a child lives with tolerance
he learns to be patient.

If a child lives with encouragement
he learns to have confidence.

If a child lives with praise
he learns to appreciate.

If a child lives with fairness
he learns justice.

If a child lives with security
he learns to have faith.

If a child lives with approval
he learns to like himself.

If a child lives with acceptance and friendship
he learns to find love in the world.

*Replace the words child/children with people or employee. Doesn't this also make sense to you?*

# 1

## Meeting Leadership Challenges in the 21st Century

*"Leadership is the art of getting someone else to do something you want done because he or she wants to do it."*

Dwight Eisenhower

The following corporate stories are indicative of the dramatic changes that have taken place regarding how companies are being managed.

> Toro Company was forced to undergo a horrific downsizing for the first time in its history. More than half of its employees lost their jobs. CEO Ken Melrose's first message to the survivors was, "We (senior management) are to blame; we've let you down; we've mismanaged the company." But Melrose believed that Toro could turn around. He transformed Toro into an open corporation by insisting that the first job of the managers was to enable their employees to be stars. He backed his words with action. Soon empowerment, cross-functional employees, the freedom to fail, team-building, structural flattening, and process-oriented work teams became the very fabric of Toro.
>
> Ken Melrose, Chairman and CEO,
> Toro Company

They brought Dee Parkinson in when the business was on the brink of extinction. After senior execs at the parent company had all but given up on Suncor's Oil Sands Group, Parkinson raised it back from the dead. She did this amazing turnaround using three simple principles: (1) go to the employees — all the employees. Ask them for help. Ask them how things can be fixed. Let them tell you how to make things right. (2) Tell them that they've told you how to fix it. Tell them in face-to-face meetings, in the employee publication, in private one-on-one meetings, everywhere. (3) Do what they've told you to do. That's it. As simple as this sounds, it saved a billion dollar oil mine from shutting down for good. This is one of the most dramatic corporate stories of the 1990s. Parkinson's courage and toughness under extreme pressure helped save a company, a town, and an industry.

> Dee Parkinson, Executive Vice President,
> Suncor Oil Sands Group

CEO Jack Stack believes that corporate problems are caused by two things: (1) no one tells employees how to make money and generate cash, and (2) management doesn't have the understanding or the fearlessness to commit to total communications. Fear of losing control and mistrust of communication cripple the company's most sincere attempts to change. He's learned that:

- A business should be run like an aquarium, so everybody can see what's going on, what's going in, what's moving around, what's coming out.
- Everything you do should be based on the understanding that job security is paramount. You should be creating a place for people to work not just this year, but for the next fifty years.

- Downsizing means that management has failed.
- You will always be more successful in business by sharing information with the people you work with than by keeping them in the dark.
- Your company will make more money if it openly shares information, ideas, and numbers.
- You can practice open-book communication and management even if you're a front-line supervisor in a company mummified in secrecy. Can these methods work? Is total communication the answer to all your company's problems?

> Jack Stack, CEO,
> Springfield Remanufacturing Co.

## Trends in the 1990s

We live in an age of unforgiving management responsibility. In the 1990s, downsizing became a troubling symbol of continuous change and relentless competition. In a recent report, "Corporate Downsizing, Job Elimination, and Job Creation," the American Management Association looked at trends in the U.S. over the last five years. Among the findings:

> In calm waters, every ship has a good captain.
> - Swedish proverb

- Even as downsizing continues, more jobs are being created. In 1995, the net change in jobs was -1.1%, a sharp improvement over the -8.4% of two years earlier. As a result, job elimination is no longer synonymous with downsizing.
- Of the new jobs created in 1995, 50.3% were hourly, 9% were middle management, and 31.1% were professional/technical.
- Middle managers, who comprise between 5% and 8% of the workforce, made up more than 15% of the laid-off workers.
- Fewer companies attribute layoffs to a short-term business downturn; more are citing long-term reasons such as improved staff utilization, re-engineering, and outsourcing.

- Fewer than half of the firms that have downsized in the past five years have subsequently increased their profits, and then only a third reported higher productivity.
- Companies that increased training budgets after downsizing were twice as likely to show profit and productivity over the long term.

## REDEFINING RELATIONSHIPS WITH EMPLOYEES

According to a CEO brief on "The People/Performance Paradox," published as a supplement to *Chief Executive Magazine* in July 1996, the 21st century will bring unprecedented challenges to face senior management, who will find themselves in a troubling paradox: at the very moment in which we need to redefine our relationship with our employees and offer them less security — we also will need more employee involvement and creativity — attributes that tend to flourish best in an atmosphere of mutual commitment and trust.

> I skate where the puck is going to be, not where it has been.
>
> - Wayne Gretzky

Study any corporation or based on your own experience, name those responsible for missed opportunities and bungled projects you have witnessed. Do management names top the list? Just ask the employees. They'll tell you that the problem definitely is management and they are the biggest barrier to change, innovation, and new ideas.

## MANAGEMENT ISN'T EASY

While management looks easy, the fact is that mediocre management is the norm. What looks easy is extraordinarily difficult. Impossible demands and high expectations are required of managers. They are expected to possess skills in finance, cost control, resource allocation,

> Teaching kids to count is fine, but teaching them what counts is best.
>
> - Bob Talbert

product development, marketing, manufacturing, and technology. They must be masters of strategy, persuasion, influence, negotiation, writing, speaking and listening, and have common sense and a positive attitude. To demonstrate leadership, managers must possess vision, involve their employees, and motivate and bring out the best in others. They are expected to be friend, mentor, and guardian of their subordinates. Not many people can live up to these expectations.

Many, however, become successful. Even though they may lack many of the skills that are part of their job descriptions, they make up for it by having "people skills." Understanding that managing involves human interactions, successful managers influence subordinates to work hard, even when they may know little about the technical aspects of the work.

> There are an enormous number of managers who have retired on the job.
>
> - Peter Drucker

Subordinates will thwart and dislike the manager who is mean-spirited, regardless of his or her technical prowess.

Great managers have the following attributes:

- They understand the importance of character.
- They are able to communicate clearly and consistently, keep promises, avoid hidden agendas, and take personal responsibility for the company's acts as well as their own.
- They empower subordinates and restrain the instinct to control.
- They create value where none exists, save and create jobs and careers.
- They exhibit more character than technical proficiency, have integrity, passion, and courage.
- They are enthusiastic and energetic.

## INVESTING IN PEOPLE SKILLS

It is easy to teach statistics, data analysis and other similar technical and business subjects but not much is being invested by corporations in "people skills" and values training. Organizations that are

> You know how leadership works... just look at how your company leader behaves.
>
> - Steven Berglas

going to survive and prosper in the future will be those that find a way to tap into the individual's human potential and explore new methods of managing, motivating and redefining the fundamental relationship between the employee and the company. To get there, managers have to create a positive, caring climate of trust in which others can be motivated to develop their intelligence and skills and be the best they can be. Trust makes cooperation possible and cooperation is especially important in an era of change and competition.

A workforce that can cooperate well with each other and with management will set a company apart from the competition. Corporations that promote people skills will be the ones who succeed. Corporations must develop the skills and behaviors needed to manage in this workplace and *change the focus from how to change employees to how to change management.*

## CHANGING MANAGEMENT BEHAVIOR

According to Francie Dalton of Dalton Alliances: "... unless and until senior management exerts the same levels of scrutiny upon management behavior as is applied to production and finance, the

> Pennies do not come from heaven. They have to be earned here on earth.
>
> - Margaret Thatcher

impact of management behavior on corporate performance will not be measurable, and therefore will remain undervalued. It is the behavior of management that stimulates or fails to stimulate discretionary energy from employees. And it is the behavior of management that establishes or shatters the *esprit de corps* in organizations — yet behavior remains a distant second to technical skills in corporate training prioritizing."

It is easy to reduce costs by cutting heads and downsizing, but it's very difficult to create value and build robust, knowledge-based organizations, especially when most people haven't been trained to do so.

## THE NEED FOR LEADERS

Corporations are looking for leaders rather than managers, i.e., people who are going to create rather than manage assets, people who can make the difficult decisions while recognizing other's feelings. Caring and sensitivity are other important qualities that will be needed to lead people. Effective leaders will derive their power from those they lead. They have to be incredibly sensitive to their subordinates and get to know them in order to build trust. Growth of companies correlates to the growth of individuals.

> There is no security on earth, only opportunity.
>
> - General Douglas MacArthur

## INVESTING IN DEVELOPING LEADERS

Making the necessary changes — shifting from a cost-cutting to a value-creation orientation, from command and control to trust — is not easy. If it were easy, everyone would be doing it. Stimulating the behaviors of learning, innovation, and trust will require existing managers to use new tools and techniques that will make many of them feel uncomfortable. And it will be difficult to give up power, structure, and authority. Many managers, who have been taught to take the workforce for granted, to see the workers on the factory floor as lazy, and low-level supervisors as not having competence and needing to be controlled, will have difficulty learning to view these same employees as assets that increase in value over time. The only thing that you have that your competition doesn't is your employees. Investing in their development will increase productivity and yield a Return on Investment (ROI) of up to 100:1.

> I believe the real difference between success and failure in a corporation can very often be traced to the question of how well the organization brings out the energies and talents of its people.
>
> - Thomas J. Watson, Jr.

It is achievable, and there are educational programs in the marketplace, such as Zig Ziglar's "Strategies For Success" training program, which is designed to help maximize competitive advantage by maximizing "people" potential. It is a values-based program that will help employees and management to develop excellence in self and others and to implement long-term voluntary behavioral change. Other valuable tools are the author's book, *Looking For The Gold*, a "how-to" book which was written to help develop personal strategies for influencing human behavior and to produce a lasting, voluntary change in behavior; and the book *Powerful Stuff*, by Rich "MR POS" Wilkins. Business will continue the process of dramatic change well into the next millennium. The needs of business will require people to be more involved, take initiative, seek responsibility, and find ways to gain cooperation of their colleagues and managers. Interpersonal skills are the tools of influence for helping others achieve goals.

> Waiting for permission is not characteristic of people who get extraordinary things done, whether leaders or individual contributors. Acting with a sense of urgency is.
>
> *The Leadership Challenge*
> by James M. Kouzes
> and Barry Z. Posner

So, how can we develop the interpersonal skills which we will absolutely need in order to maximize our ability to lead others into the 21st century? That is what this book is all about... developing interpersonal skills and building effective leaders.

## Lesson in Leadership

There is no doubt in my mind that companies will continue to want to grow as we approach the next millennium and are already beginning to reinvest in their employees in order to increase their productivity. Companies will also focus more on management behavior, similar to what has been applied to production and finance, since employees take their behavioral lessons from the top.

Aspiring leaders in the 21st century will be expected to do more and be committed to the success of others. In making decisions, they will learn to look at more than one factor and take into consideration the needs and interests of ALL their constituents. People skills and other behavioral indicators such as employee development and the ability to cooperate with others will become standard in evaluating managerial performance.

## VIEWS ON LEADERSHIP AND LEADERS

Leadership is the art of getting others to do something you want done because they want to do it.

Leadership is an attitude (before it becomes an ability).

Leadership grows out of the values the leader holds (open-minded, kind, caring, considerate, etc.).

Leadership enlivens management and gives managers a reason to go forward.

Leadership is the art of instilling in people the attitudes and feelings that they can and will accomplish objectives that enhance their personal and professional lives.

Leadership — the capacity to influence others.

Leaders create environments where people want to do their best work.

Leaders get their authority from below; managers get their authority from above.

Leaders motivate by example.

Leaders earn trust when it becomes clear that they are not going to dominate and harm employees.

Leaders are sincere and genuinely concerned about people and how they respond to work, other members of the workforce, and CHANGE.

Leaders lead change.

Leaders look for strengths in people, not their weaknesses.

A leader is someone who has followers.

Leaders help people reach their full potential.

A leader brings out the best in people.

Leaders derive their power from those they lead.

Leaders create rather than manage assets.

Great leaders with shared vision and motivated people equal great companies where customers, employees, and stockholders are happy.

A creative leader is one who recognizes the tremendous potential in people and strives to establish and maintain a climate where individuals may develop and maximize their contributions through teamwork.

Your job as a leader is to grow others.

Leaders create voluntary change in employee behavior.

Leaders are learners, able to acknowledge mistakes and change their behavior accordingly.

No matter how you cut it, it comes down to how to deal with people.

A leader's major goal is mastering the mechanics of teamwork.

# SUCCESS STORIES

## Wisdom on Work

Thomas Alva Edison was once quoted as saying, "I am wondering what would have happened to me if some fluent talker had converted me to the theory of the eight-hour day, and convinced me that it was not fair to my fellow workers to put forth my best efforts in my work. I am glad that the eight-hour day had not been invented when I was a young man. If my life had been made up of eight-hour days, I do not believe I could have accomplished a great deal. This country would not amount to as much as it does if the young men had been afraid that they might earn more than they were paid."

Edison believed that rewarding efforts called for 2% inspiration and 98% perspiration.

David Livingston activated this work philosophy. He worked in a factory from 6:00 a.m. until 8:00 p.m. Then he attended night school for two hours, followed by studying far into the night. It could be said Livingston's accomplishments were the result of inspired perspiration.

Leonardo Da Vinci understood the need for hard work as well as the benefits involved. "Thou, Oh God, doth send to us all good things you hope for. A man who's afraid of hard work better be brave enough to accept poverty."

The honey bee provides a splendid example, visiting 125 clover heads to make one gram of honey. That means 3 million trips to make one pound of honey.

Michelangelo disputed the wonder of his own talent by saying, "If people knew how hard I have had to work to gain my mastery, it wouldn't seem wonderful at all."

*Is it any wonder than ancient and present sages suggest that success is always preceded by hard work?*

*- The Speaker's Sourcebook*

## Why Work Hard?

IBM is a model for walking the talk of their mission. Author Charles Garfield once gave a series of lectures at several IBM facilities around the world. When he asked IBM employees about their mission, everyone told him: to provide the "best customer service in the world."

He was most impressed, however, late one day when he was leaving a meeting room in Austin, Texas. He happened to notice a maintenance man sweeping his heart out.

So Garfield tried his usual question. The man looked puzzled by the word "mission," so he rephrased the question, asking "Why do you work so hard? Is your boss around here?"

"No," he replied.

Garfield tried again, "Isn't he going to come in here tomorrow morning and check how well you swept up?"

"No," was the answer.

So Garfield asked again, "Then why are you working so hard?"

The man looked perplexed at this foolish question, and said, "Why? Because our customers come here, and you might be one of them."

*- Burr Ridge, IL. Cited by the Pryor Report,*
Clemson, SC

## Persistence Pays Off

Once upon a time, there was a Louisville University quarterback, who had a dream, an obsession. His dream was to play pro football. However, upon graduation, this young quarterback was not drafted by the pros.

He did not give up. He wrote to several teams and finally got a tryout with the Steelers. He gave it his best shot but did not make even the third string.

"You got a raw deal," "It wasn't meant to be," "I guess it's time to hang it up," his friends told him. But the young athlete did not hang it up. Continuing to knock on doors and write letters, he finally received another invitation. Again, he did not make the team.

Most people would have given up long before this, but not this determined young man. He was fanatically committed to his personal dream. From his early days of playing sandlot football, through his success in high school and college football, he had hung tight to his goal.

Patiently and persistently, he continued to pursue tryouts with pro teams. He finally went to Baltimore and made the team. Training and working long hours on fitness and skill, he worked his way from third string to becoming known as the greatest quarterback in the NFL.

Who was this persistent goal-seeker? You guessed it — the dreamer was Johnny Unitas!

*- The Speaker's Sourcebook*

## Half A Stroke

During one year in the 1960s, near the peak of his skills, golfer Jack Nicklaus earned approximately $400,000 on the PGA tour.

Another golfer on the tour that year was Bob Charles. As a professional, he was not as successful as Jack Nicklaus. During the same year, Bob Charles earned approximately $40,000 on the PGA tour, one-tenth that of Jack Nicklaus (excluding income from endorsements and other revenue-generating activities).

It might surprise you to learn that the difference in their respective per round stroke average was less than half a stroke. Imagine that!

The difference between the greatest golfer of all time and a very good golfer was less than half a stroke per round.

- Paul S. Goldner in *Red Hot Cold Call Selling,*
American Management Association

# 2

## The Winner's Triangle

*"No one can make you feel inferior without your consent."*

Eleanor Roosevelt

### THE DIFFERENCE BETWEEN MANAGEMENT AND LEADERSHIP

People have a tendency to use the terms leadership and management interchangeably, but they do have different meanings. Leaders get their authority from below; managers get theirs from above. Leadership requires interacting with people and inspiring them to be the best that they can be. Leaders lead people; managers lead things and projects. Henry Ford once defined a friend as "someone who brings out the best in you." Isn't that what leaders really do, or what they should do?

Leadership is the art of instilling the attitudes and feelings in people so that they can and will accomplish objectives that enhance their personal and professional lives. Great leaders with shared vision and motivated people equal great companies where customers, employees, and stockholders are happy. These are the essential elements of a winning team or a successful company. Please note the addition of the word *employee* in this statement.

The tragic waste in the U.S. is not our wasting of natural resources but our wasting of human resources. The greatest

15

untapped natural resource and most expensive in any organization is people. The average person in this country works at less than 50% of capacity. Motivating people to their full potential is the quickest way a manager can multiply his or her full personal effectiveness and become a leader. Employees are just waiting for someone to come along and bring out the best in them, which will result in productivity increases of 10, 20, 30, or even 100%.

---

### MANAGEMENT
*The skill of attaining pre-determined objectives with and through the voluntary cooperation of others.*

### LEADERSHIP
*The art of instilling in people the attitudes and feelings that they can and will accomplish objectives that enhance their personal and professional lives.*

---

## CREATIVE LEADERSHIP

Successful companies are those whose leaders create positive, caring environments where employees feel terrific about themselves. Don't you agree that people who feel good about themselves produce more and better work? Everything rises and falls on leaders, who get their authority from below and are totally committed to

> **Y**ou must be able to underwrite the honest mistakes of your subordinates if you wish to develop their initiative and experience.
>
> - Bruce Clarke, U.S. General

building better people. A creative leader is one who recognizes the tremendous potential in people and strives to establish and maintain a climate

> **I**f you consistently do your best, the worst won't happen.
>
> - B. C. Forbes

where individuals may develop and maximize their contributions. Within this creative environment, they share their vision and involve others in the process of identifying and pursuing meaningful goals that bring both short-term and long-run benefits to all. The cornerstones of a creative climate are mutual trust, respect, and commitment. A creative leader must be honest, open, and sharing, if mutual trust and respect are to be cultivated.

What does it take to be a creative leader? Based on recent surveys of more than 15,000 people, the top four characteristics of admired leaders and the percentage of people who selected them are:

1. Being honest   87%
2. Being forward-looking or visionary   71%
3. Being inspirational   68%
4. Being competent   58%

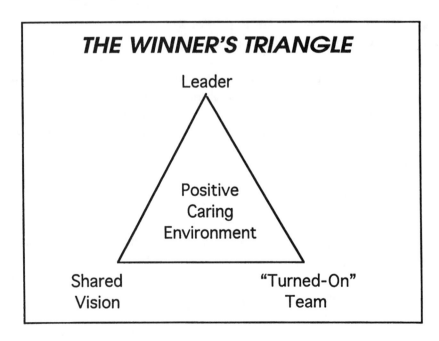

## THE WINNER'S TRIANGLE

Leader

Positive
Caring
Environment

Shared
Vision

"Turned-On"
Team

**Honest leaders** are credible, which earns them the trust and confidence of their people.

**Visionary leaders** share their vision, communicate, and involve their people who want to know where the organization wants to go and how they fit in; determine what is acceptable behavior; their roles and responsibilities; how they can contribute and what is expected of them.

**Inspirational leaders** motivate others generally by example and practice the "Three R's of Management" (they consistently recognize, reward, and reinforce people, often publicly).

**Competent leaders** are respected by everyone.

**Credible leaders** have other characteristics as well:

- They do what they say they'll do
- Their actions are consistent with the wishes of the people they lead
- They believe in the self-worth of others
- They are capable of making a difference in the lives of others
- They admit mistakes and foster the notion "it's okay to make mistakes"
- They arouse optimism in others
- They create a climate for learning

I believe that a leader is like a friend, someone who brings out the best in you. A leader has the ability to develop people to their full potential, which not only ensures personal growth, but also translates into business success. Individual growth and business success are inseparable. We individually take responsibility to develop our knowledge, talents, and skills to their full potential to increase our value and contribution to the success of our business and to our personal growth. Growth and development are a shared responsibility of both leadership and the individual.

**N**o structure in the world... can ever substitute for the innovative leader, the individual inspired by vision or even by fear, who can instill a sense of urgency and a demand for change throughout an organization.

- *The Boundaryless Organization*

## DEVELOPING GREAT WORKPLACES

As leaders, our job is to individually and collectively create and maintain a positive, caring workplace environment. Successful people understand the value of surrounding themselves with other successful/positive people in an environment conducive to maximum productivity and quality.

> How could you hit a target you don't have?
>
> - Zig Ziglar

A positive, caring environment:

- Allows people to rise to the level of others around them
- Inspires people to achieve more
- Empowers people naturally
- Gives people more confidence in that it builds people up rather than tears them down
- Helps people overcome their fears, or at the very least, to deal with failure and learn from it
- Reinforces our strengths
- Helps people understand the importance of helping/mentoring others
- Builds trust, communication, loyalty, self-esteem, and relationships with others

It is amazing what people can do if they are treated with respect, encouraged to do their best, are appreciated, and work in a positive, caring environment. Study after study has indicated results showing up to 300% increase in productivity when employees feel that they are important. Investing in people pays off — why aren't we doing it more? As a side benefit, customer service also improves because employees generally treat their customers in the same manner as they are treated.

Learn to tap the greatest untapped and most expensive resource that we have available to us. The average person works at less than 50% of his or her

> The greatest thing in this world is not so much where we are, but in what direction we are moving.
>
> - Oliver Wendell Holmes, Jr.

> **A**lso worth remembering is that in any man's dark hour, a pat on the back and an earnest handclasp may work a small miracle.
>
> - S.L.A. Marshall, U.S. General

potential. The only thing that we have that our competitors don't is our people. Developing people to be the best that they could be, using the abilities that they have, or can acquire to their fullest, is the key.

What qualities do successful companies look for the most in new employees? Overwhelmingly, the most essential quality is *attitude*. Employees want people who are willing to put their hearts in their work, cooperate as part of a team, feel good about themselves, and are self-motivated. These traits are characteristic of positive people.

Nothing constructive can be accomplished without a positive attitude. There are two quotes I like to use when illustrating the importance of having a positive attitude. One is from Henry Ford: "Give me the I CAN over the IQ *every* time." The other is from Harry Truman, "The world is run by 'C' students." The neat thing is that a positive attitude can be taught, especially in caring environments.

Caring seems to have nearly disappeared in the business world in the 1990s. A negative business climate and downsizing has created negative, noncaring environments and although short-term corporation profits have been higher, employees distrust management and employee loyalty has been significantly affected. We

> **Y**ou cannot push anyone up the ladder unless he is willing to climb himself.
>
> - Andrew Carnegie

absolutely need to rebuild and renew caring in the workplace. *People don't care how much you know until they know how much you care.* You demonstrate caring by helping people accomplish their goals and objectives. Zig Ziglar says, *"You can have everything in life you want if you will just help enough other people get what they want."*

Keep these leadership principles in mind when developing training programs for your company. Excellent people skills are very important and will go a long way toward your and your department's success.

# Complete Building Services

## WE AT CBS BELIEVE THAT:

1. All employees are responsible, thinking adults who inherently want to do their best.

2. Human resources are too valuable to waste or to leave untapped.

3. Creative talent and skills are widely distributed at all levels of an organization.

4. Employees will surface important problems and concerns if they feel the organization will respond appropriately.

5. Work is more interesting when people are challenged in performing it.

6. People take pride in training others.

7. Better performance occurs when artificial differences in how people are treated are removed.

8. Real responsibility motivates high performance.

9. People make better decisions, and implement them better, when they work together.

## A Leadership Formula

| Inspiring Leader | Coercing Boss |
| --- | --- |
| ■ Rewards | Threatens |
| ■ Encourages | Finds fault |
| ■ Listens | Talks |
| ■ Keeps employees informed | Keeps them guessing |
| ■ Stimulates others to think | Wants to do all the thinking |
| ■ Tells why and what to do | Tells others how to do it |
| ■ Helps others solve problems | Ignores others' problems |
| ■ Wants long-run loyalty | Wants prompt obedience |
| ■ Caring | Blunt |
| ■ Tries persuasion | Flaunts authority |
| ■ Employee-centered | Production-centered |
| ■ Assumes best in others | Assumes worst in people |
| ■ Gives a square deal | Takes advantage of others |
| ■ High-minded | Vulgar-minded |
| ■ Considers before acting | Impulsive |
| ■ Appreciative | Thankless |

# SUCCESS STORIES

## A Winner in the Game of Life

He was an unknown when his first book was published in 1936. He had been a successful salesman but was determined to teach people what he felt were important principles in the world of human relations and public speaking. Leaving Warrensburg, Missouri, he approached the directors of the Twenty-Third Street YMCA in New York with his dream for teaching. The course was untried and unknown, so the directors were wary of its possibility for success. Finally, they agreed to pay him on a commission basis.

Within a few years, the course was so popular that the young man was making $30 a night in commission rather than the usual $2 teaching fee. While teaching in Larchmont, New York, he met a publishing executive who had enrolled in the course. The publisher was so impressed with the material that he suggested the instructor gather it into a book. And that he did.

After this young man, Dale Carnegie was his name, published *How To Win Friends and Influence People,* it stayed on the *New York Times* best-seller list for ten straight years. No other author can claim such an accomplishment. The final numbers are not yet in, but more than 10 million copies have been sold, and an additional 200,000 copies are purchased every year.

Voltaire said, "Life is like a game of cards. Each player must accept the cards that life deals to him or her. With cards in hand, each person must decide how the hand will be played in order to win the game." Dale Carnegie understood the necessity to play the hand he had been dealt. It would certainly be fair to say that Dale Carnegie was successful in the card game of life.

*- The Speaker's Sourcebook*

## What You See is What You Get

Robert Woodruff, president of Coca-Cola from 1923 to 1955, boldly said during World War II: "We will see that every man in uniform gets a bottle of Coca-Cola for five cents wherever he is and whatever it costs." After World War II ended, he said that in his lifetime he wanted everyone in the world to have tasted Coca-Cola. Quite a vision!

Walt Disney had died when Disney World first opened, so his widow was asked to speak. She was introduced by a man who said, "Mrs. Disney, I just wish Walt could have seen this." She stood up, then simply said, "He did," and sat down. Visions are powerful.

Remember, many great achievers began life in the poorest of homes, with little education, and few advantages: Thomas Edison was a newsboy on trains. Andrew Carnegie started work at $4 a month, John D. Rockefeller at $6 a week. Abraham Lincoln was born in a log cabin. Charles Dickens was lame. Homer was blind. What gave these great individuals the stamina to overcome severe setbacks and become successful? Each had an inner dream that lit a fire that could not be extinguished.

*- The Working Communicator*

## Who Defines Customer Service?
## The Customer, That's Who

The year before Jan Carlzon took over Scandinavian Airline System (SAS), the carrier suffered an $8 million loss. The year before that it was $20 million in the hole. The year after Carlzon took the reins, SAS turned a profit of $72 million and didn't look back. What made the difference? Carlzon maintains that the key was to move customer service to the front line, to employees who have direct contact with the public, rather than have it defined by marketing. Explaining the switch, the CEO noted: "Last year, each of our 10 million customers came in contact with approximately five SAS employees, and this contact lasted an average of 15 seconds each time. Thus, SAS is created in the minds of our customers 50 million times a year, 15 at a time. These 50 million 'moments of truth' are the moments that ultimately determine whether SAS will succeed or fail as a company. They are the moments when we must prove to our customers that SAS is their best alternative."

It is those 50 million "moments of truth" that make the difference. SAS offers superb customer service because it fully recognizes that the customer is the one who defines customer service.

*- The Speaker's Sourcebook*

## The Challenging Spirit

Coupled with Honda's vision is a unique credo that we call the "challenging spirit." Throughout our history, most of Honda's great achievements are a result of accepting new challenges from the competitive market or challenges that ensue from government regulation.

Let me give you one of the earliest examples of how this challenging spirit works. In March 1954, Mr. Honda stood on a small wooden box in the back of the factory and told his employees that the company would enter a race against the world's best motorcycles on the Isle of Man in Great Britain. At that time, this event was the most competitive and prestigious race in the world. Not only would we enter, Mr. Honda said, we would win.

Now, that may not sound like an unusual goal for a motorcycle company. But at the time, our engines were only a third as powerful as the European bikes that dominated racing. Our company was very new and very small. It was an outrageous declaration. A seemingly insurmountable task.

But win we did. For seven years, the company's energies, resources and pride were massed toward this commitment. And, in 1961, when Honda motorcycles took first, second, third, fourth, and fifth place on the Isle of Man, we had achieved more than just preeminence in engineering. The challenging spirit was alive and each of our employees had developed a true global viewpoint.

- Osmau Lido,
Honda North America

## Express Your Faith

Tell a child, a husband, or an employee that he is stupid or dumb at a certain thing, that he has no gift for it, and that he is doing it all wrong and you have destroyed almost every incentive to try to improve. But use the opposite technique; be liberal with encouragement; make the thing seem easy to do; let the other person know that you have faith in his ability to do it, that he has an undeveloped flair for it — and he will practice until the dawn comes in at the window in order to excel.

- Dale Carnegie

## Worth A Million

When asked why he was worth $3,000 a day or $1 million a year in salary, Charles M. Schwab responded, "I consider my ability to arouse enthusiasm among men the greatest asset I possess, and the way to develop the best that is in a man is to be appreciative and to encourage, so I am anxious to praise but loathe to find fault. If I like anything, I am hearty in my appreciation and lavish in my praise."

In a later interview, responding to a comparable question about his success, Schwab reiterated his conviction. "In my wide association in life, meeting with many and great men in various parts of the world," Schwab declared, "I have yet to find a man, however great or exalted his station, who did no better work and put forth greater effort under the spirit of approval than he would ever do under a spirit of criticism."

- *The Speaker's Sourcebook*

## Visualize Your Vision

Author Irving Stone dedicated a lifetime to studying the lives of great people. He is renowned for having written novelized biographies of men such as Charles Darwin, Sigmund Freud, Vincent van Gogh, and Michelangelo.

Stone was once asked if any similarities or common characteristics were predominant in the lives of these successful people. He responded, "The people I write about, sometime in their life, have a vision or dream of something they believe should be accomplished and they commit themselves to it."

"These people are beaten over the head, knocked down, vilified, and for years they get nowhere. But every time they're knocked down, they stand back up. They cannot be destroyed. At the end of their lives, they've accomplished some modest part of what they set out to do."

*- The Speaker's Sourcebook*

## A True Leader

In an issue of *Life* magazine, James F. Hind, author of *The Heart and Soul of Effective Management: A Christian Approach to Managing and Motivating People,* gave this assessment of Christ's prowess as the Chief Executive:

"In only three years He defined a mission and formed strategies to carry it out. With a staff of 12 unlikely men, He organized Christianity, which today has branches in all the world's countries and a 32.4% share of the world's population, twice as big as its nearest rival. Leaders want to develop people to their full potential, taking ordinary people and making them extraordinary. This is what Christ did with His disciples. Jesus was the most effective executive in history. The results He achieved are second to none."

## Winners vs. Losers

Winners say, "If it is to be, it is up to me."
    Losers say, "I can't help it."
Winners translate dreams into reality.
    Losers translate reality into dreams.
Winners empower.
    Losers control.
Winners say, "Let's find out."
    Losers say, "Nobody knows."
Winners are not afraid of losing.
    Losers are afraid of winning.
Winners work harder than losers.
    Losers are always too busy.
Winners say, "I was wrong."
    Losers say, "It was not my fault."
Winners want to.
    Losers have to.
Winners always make time.
    Losers often waste time.
Winners make commitments.
    Losers make promises.
Winners say, "I'll *plan* to do that."
    Losers say, "I'll *try* to do that."
Winners say, "I'm good but not as good as I can be."
    Losers say, "I'm not as bad as a lot of other people."
Winners listen to what others say.
    Losers wait until it's their turn to talk.
Winners catch others doing things right.
    Losers catch others doing things wrong.
Winners learn from others.
    Losers resent their colleagues.
Winners see opportunities.
    Losers see only the problems.
Winners do it.
    Losers talk about it.
Winners feel responsible for more than their jobs.
    Losers frequently state, I only work here.

Winners say, There ought to be a better way.

Losers say, That's the way it's always been done.

Winners celebrate others.

Losers complain about others.

Winners are willing to pay the price.

Losers expect it on a silver platter.

Winners always expect success.

Losers always expect failure.

by Wolf Rinke

# 3

---

# Begin at the Beginning, with a Positive Attitude

*"Keep looking for the gold in others and you'll always find some in you."*

A.S. Migs Damiani

*Leadership is an attitude before it becomes an ability.* So are the 30 most frequently named qualities of successful individuals. Your attitude makes all the difference in how you approach your work, how hard you work, and ultimately, how successful you are.

## YOUR ATTITUDE MAKES A DIFFERENCE

Attitude isn't simply a state of mind... it is also a reflection of what we value. Attitude is more than just saying "I can," it is believing you can. It requires believing before seeing, because seeing is based on circumstances, believing is based on faith. Attitude is so contagious especially when we allow it to turn our doubts of the past into passions of today and set the stage for our tomorrows. We have total ownership of our attitudes. No one else has the power to alter our attitudes without our permission. Our attitude allows us to become more empowering than money, to rise above our failures, and accept others for who they are, and what they say. It is more important than giftedness and is the forerunner of all skills needed for happiness and success. Our attitudes can be used to build us up or put us down — the choice is ours. It also gives us the wisdom to know that we can't change events of the past. I am convinced that life is 10% what happens to me, and 90% how I respond to it... and it is with this state of mind that I remain in charge of my ATTITUDES.

- Rich "MR POS" Wilkins

Everyone wants to be successful; however, few people truly become successful. Look around you and name people and organizations that you consider successful and you will find that they *all* have positive attitudes. Listen carefully to those who succeed as they credit attitude, not aptitude, as the significant difference behind their success. We live in a negative world. By the time a person reaches age 18 she/he has heard the words "no," "don't," and "can't" over 148,000 times. Ninety percent of the input in our mind is negative and coincidentally, ninety percent of us also expect to do poorly. That makes it easier for individuals with a positive attitude, and who raise the level of their expectations, to do well in life. People get in life what they expect. Could you imagine how much better this world would be if people were positive and raised their level of productivity just one notch?

> If it is to be, it is up to me.
> - William H. Johnson

## THE IMPORTANCE OF A POSITIVE ATTITUDE

Zig Ziglar often refers to a recent study which disclosed that there was no direct correlation found between high school valedictorians and success. Does that surprise you? If attitude were taught to these students in the home and school and the same results were found, would that

> You must believe to achieve.

also be surprising? It would to me. In Japan, one hour of every school day (for 3- to 18-year olds) is spent on developing good attitudes and, in the home, children are encouraged to be the best that they can be. Is it any wonder why Japan has become a very successful nation?

The opposite of success is not failure. It is conformance. Failure is the foundation for success — it is an event, not a person. We have two choices available to us. We can accept things as they are, or become agents for change. In order for change to occur, *you* must make a decision to change, be committed, and be trained. Training helps change behavioral patterns.

> **P**ositive thinking won't let you do anything but it will let you do everything better than negative thinking. It will let you use your abilities.
>
> - Zig Ziglar

Positive attitude is the result of new thinking — believing in yourself, focusing on successes, learning from failure, and surrounding yourself with people who share your values, principles, and thinking.

Zig Ziglar, widely reputed to be the world's best teacher of motivation, credits attitude to be much more important than aptitude. He supports his conviction on hundreds of studies that show that:

- 85% of why you got your job, why you keep your job, and why you get promoted is POSITIVE ATTITUDE.
- 98% of why people get fired is BAD ATTITUDE.
- 68% of why customers change vendors and contractors is BAD ATTITUDE.

Companies rise and fall in their customers' favor for a variety of reasons. The American Society for Quality Control reports

> **I**t is amazing what we can accomplish if we only begin.

the following study showing the relative importance of reasons companies lose customers:

| Reason | % |
|--------|---|
| Die | 1 |
| Moved away | 3 |
| Influenced by friends | 5 |
| Lured away by the competition | 9 |
| Dissatisfied with product | 14 |
| Turned away by an attitude of indifference on the part of a company employee | 68 |

The emphasis on good service has increased so much of late that the ASQC warns: "Unless a customer is completely satisfied — to the point of being positively delighted and willing to brag about the product or service received — there exists great potential for market damage and future trouble for the company."

Do you think having a positive attitude is important?

## FOUNDATION FOR SUCCESS

In Zig Ziglar's books and seminars, he cites the thirty qualities of success which were selected by thousands of people, who were asked to name the traits in people that they admire and attribute to their success. These include:

### Qualities of Success

| | | |
|---|---|---|
| Honest | Common sense | Character |
| Enthusiastic | Hard-working | Dedicated |
| Positive mental attitude | Self-respect | Humble |
| Confident | Loving | Organized |
| Discipline | Humor | Good listener |
| Persistent | Friendly | Communicator |
| Loyal | Motivated | Learner |
| Faith | Compassionate | Empathy |
| Goals | Integrity | Dependable |
| Patient | Decisive | Knowledge |

Examine these qualities closely and you'll see that nearly all of them are attitudes or involve attitude. They can all be taught; therefore, they can become skills. Imagine if your employees were taught these qualities. Would they be able to increase their oppor-

> Nothing can stop the man with the right mental attitude from achieving his goal; nothing on earth can help the man with the wrong mental attitude.
>
> - W.W. Ziege

tunities and be more successful? Of course they would. What if your children were taught these qualities, or your spouse? Would family life and school life be enhanced? Of course they would. Why then, are we not teaching these qualities in our homes — and in our schools? Ziglar says the most important lesson we can learn is that we already have portions of every quality of success within us and we need to develop and/or reinforce those which need strengthening.

I recall an employee once telling me that I could not change his attitude. I responded, "You are right, I cannot change your attitude. However, the exciting thing is that you could and I am going to teach you how." About eighteen months later, the same employee received a Golden Attitude Award, recognizing the improvement he made. Positive attitudes are contagious and can be taught. If management is positive and upbeat, what is the likelihood that their employees are also positive? You can bet that the probability is high.

Is attitude important? Francis X. Maguire, while a Senior Vice President of Federal Express, helped Federal Express become America's first winner of the Malcolm Baldrige National Quality Award in the category of service. In 1990, he said at a national engineering conference that ATTITUDE would become the management chal-

> The last, if not the greatest, of all human freedoms: To choose your own "attitude".
>
> - Bruno Betteheim

lenge of the 1990s. Many of America's companies who were committed to Total Quality programs in the 1990s now train their managers in ATTITUDE. *They have found that change in management attitude is a key in improving a company's performance.* ATTITUDE reflects values, which is what drives and organizes people. It is what a company/department/individual stands for, it is what people believe in. It is crucial to competitive success — it *is* Total Quality Management (TQM).

## FOUR A'S OF SUCCESS

The Four A's of Success are: attitude, aptitude, attendance, and appearance.

- Studies have shown that **attitude** is responsible for about 85% of people's success. Is attitude important? CEOs say it's all in the attitude. When asked to rank the factors that influenced their climb up the corporate ladder, personal drive, and ambition was the number one factor, followed closely by personal values.

- **Aptitude,** which includes background, and education and experience is sometimes an accurate predictor of performance once he or she makes it to the top, but is not perceived as important on the way up the ladder.

- **Attendance** is a large part of "doing the job." If you were hiring someone, would you choose an applicant who had missed 3 days of work during the past year or 23 days? No matter how qualified someone is, attendance and/or tardiness will affect their productivity and promotability.

- **Appearance** is also an important factor in one's success, not so much how someone looks, but whether or not they are well-dressed, neat, clean, and presentable. Zig Ziglar tells the story of running across a young man who wore his hair similar to Bart Simpson of television fame. Zig said that he would go to war over the young man's right to wear his hair any way he wanted, but he would not hire him.

*Success is not measured against others. It is based on what you could have done with what you've got.* Success is saying each day, "today I'm going to give it my best shot" and "knowing at the end of the day that you have done your best."

Rich "MR POS" Wilkins, in his book *Powerful Stuff,* says your attitude isn't a state of mind, it's a reflection of what you value. Take a look at the following model:

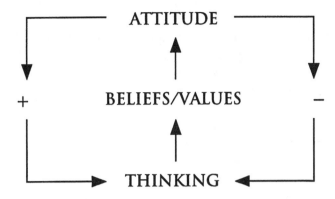

Our attitude, positive or negative, is a reflection of what we believe and value, which comes from the way we think. Norman Vincent Peale said, *"Change the way you think, and you can change the world."* Nothing positive can be accomplished without thinking positively. Change what goes into your mind and you can change your attitude. Associate with positive people, listen to motivational tapes and read lots of success stories. These ideas will help you open your mind to new ways of thinking and a positive attitude.

> **A**lways bear in mind that your own resolution to succeed is more important than any other one thing.
>
> - Abraham Lincoln

## POSITIVE LEADERS

- have positive attitudes
- are achievers
- have goals
- teach/coach others
- are inspiring
- are finders (look for the "gold" in others)
- communicate a lot and communicate well (face to face)
- confront problems
- greet others enthusiastically
- believe in themselves and others
- have exceptional work habits

- share their experiences
- listen down and get their authority from below
- smile a lot and say "thank you"
- welcome constructive criticism
- reward, give credit to others
- make mistakes and benefit from them
- always take the extra step(s)
- assume the best in people
- show appreciation
- are kind, honest and proud
- are caring and considerate
- don't point fingers
- tell *why* and *how*
- use persuasion
- are team players/builders
- are mentors/trainers
- place others' needs before their own
- criticize performance, while praising the performer
- earn the respect of their peers and subordinates
- make others feel important
- are change agents.

# Leo Houser's
# ATTITUDES ARE EVERYTHING

## 17 Necessary Ingredients For Being Effective With People

You will get what you want out of life only if you are able to get along with people. Getting along with others means that they like you and will do things for you. In other words, they respond positively to your personality. Your personality is nothing more than attitudes in action. It is the way you communicate your

> **A** strong, positive self image is the best possible preparation for success in life.
>
> - Dr. Joyce Brothers

thoughts about others and yourself. Here are some pointers to remember to make your personality pleasing, one that creates positive actions in others:

1. To have a friend, you must be one.
2. The greatest hunger that people have is to be needed, wanted, and loved. Help create those feelings in others.
3. Don't try to impress others. Let them impress you.
4. Be kind to people. You can't always love them, but you can be kind to them.
5. Learn to like yourself. Others will respond to you the way you respond to yourself.
6. Be enthusiastic. Nothing significant was ever achieved without enthusiasm — including deep, rich human relationships.
7. Be positive. Positive people attract others; negative people repel others.
8. Do things to make people feel important. Write a letter. Give a compliment. Say, "thank you." *Praise, encourage, support, cooperate.*
9. Sticking up for your "rights" is great, but do you always have to be right? Letting the other person be right once in a while will keep friendships warm.
10. Be a good listener. You can have a greater effect on others by the way you listen than by the way you talk.
11. Unless you can say something worthy about a person, say nothing.
12. Call a person by name, use it often in conversation.
13. Communicate cheerfulness. Smile. Be pleasant. Talk about the brighter things in life.
14. Avoid arguments.
15. If you're going to make fun of someone, make sure it's you.
16. Help people help themselves. The greatest compliment someone can give you is to say, "I like myself better when I'm with you."
17. Be genuinely interested in others. Get them to talk about themselves. Ask for their opinions, ideas, viewpoints.

# A Proven Success Formula

Interviews with successful people indicate that having and maintaining a positive attitude by far heads the list of winning qualities. Dale Carnegie claimed 85% of your success is related to attitude and nothing constructive could be done without having a positive attitude. How can you develop a winning attitude?

**A**    associate with positive people • always make today your best day • accept 100% responsibility • always do what you feel is the right thing to do • ask questions

**T**    treat others with respect • treat employees as if they were your friends • treat employees as appreciating assets • treat employees as if they were what they ought to be and could be

**T**    TRY, TRY, TRY — never quit trying • take pride in a job well done • talk like a winner • be THANKFUL

**I**    isolate negative thoughts • improve interpersonal skills • invest in training • improve communication skills • inspire people to do their best and achieve more • involve employees

**T**    THINK like a winner. Change the way you think by opening your mind to positive input. • TRUST others • be Teachable • turn the other cheek

**U**    utilize your God-given talent daily • unlock your inborn creativity

**D**    don't be afraid to make mistakes • dream big dreams • do what you love to do • develop a reputation for speed and dependability • develop resiliency and bounce back • develop a workaholic mentality • do the job right the first time • be Decisive • have Desire. Be persistent and determined • do more than you are paid to do • be a Difference-maker in the lives of others • * do unto others as they would like done unto them

**E**    expect positive outcomes of yourself and others and raise the quality bar each time • expect the best • be Enthusiastic and optimistic • lead by Example • empower deserving employees • enhance your people skills • encourage employees to reach their full potential • establish and maintain a positive workplace • earn other people's respect

**S**    speak well of others. Look for the gold. • smile • serve others • show you care • set and achieve goals • strive for excellence • start now!

Remember, you can have everything in life you want if you'll only help other people get what they want.

\* The Platinum Rule by Tony Allesandra

## Lesson in Leadership

Once we are aware and have a complete understanding that a positive attitude is absolutely essential in order to reach our goals, we will develop/reinforce our attitudes. Everything begins as an attitude — including quality, leadership, and communicating — before it becomes a skill. It isn't easy being optimistic every day of your life, but it is important that your employees perceive you to be inspiring and continually looking after their interests.

All too often, people condition themselves into a stifling pool of "mediocrity" because they don't have positive expectations of themselves. Leaders are expected to raise their own expectations and the expectations of others. With a positive attitude, you are more likely to make better decisions because positive thinking opens up your mind and offers new options.

Aptitude gets you the interview. Attitude gets you the job and promotions. It can also get you fired.

Success = Aptitude + Attitude

## SUCCESS STORIES

### I Am Somebody

If I try, I can do it all,
Pull myself up, whenever I fall,
Be anything I want to be,
But first, I have to learn to be me!
I will learn as I go along,
To correct mistakes when I do wrong,
Believe in myself, and others I'll lead.
With a positive attitude, I will succeed.

- Jaime Grable

## Positive Self Image

When I think of self image, I think of the story of a lion. Each day he would stand at the crossroads of the jungle. As the animals fled by, he would ask each one the same question: "Who's the king of the jungle?" And each day the animals would all give the same answer, "The lion is!" The lion would smile and the animals would continue on their way.

One day, an elephant came by. The lion bellowed out his usual question, "Who's the king of the jungle?" Now the elephant had heard about the lion's daily routine. And frankly, he didn't like it. So he decided he would not answer the lion's question. He would dramatize it.

He took his trunk, wrapped it around the lion's body, whirled the lion in the air, and threw him against the trunk of a huge oak tree. The lion hit the trunk with a "thud" and came crashing down to the ground in a heap. After a minute, the bewildered lion raised his head, blinked his eyes, and said to the elephant: "Well, you didn't have to get mad about it, just because you didn't know the answer." Now that lion had a positive self image!

*- Rev. Mark Link, S.J.,*
*Facilitating the Student's Self Image*

## Be Positive

If someone offered you $10 million in cash if you would consistently show a positive attitude for the next 30 days, would you give it a try? If they defined such an attitude as "acting positive, pleasant, friendly, enthusiastic, and encouraging," could you do that for 30 days? I think you could. You would have a good attitude for a month, because you would be highly motivated to win the prize money. Now, nobody is going to offer you such a cash prize for a good attitude, but the real-life payoffs for a positive attitude are outstanding! They include:

- **Happiness.** The better your attitude the happier you will be! Happiness is not a commodity that is found by pursuit. Instead, it is a state of mind produced by a positive attitude.
- **Health.** A good attitude is a better pain reliever than Anacin, Tylenol, Mediprin, and Bayer, all put together! A positive mental attitude strengthens the body's immune system and releases a natural drug (more powerful than morphine) into the mind.
- **Self-confidence.** A good attitude causes people to feel good about themselves and project that feeling to others.
- **Better relationships.** People who feel good about themselves are not on the defensive with other people. They are open and honest and have rich, rewarding relationships.
- **Improved performance.** Experts say that attitude accounts for 75% of all job success. People perform better in every area of their lives with a good attitude than they do with a bad one!
- **Encouragement for other people.** Since attitude is highly contagious, your good attitude will automatically make you a real benefit to everyone you meet.
- **Increased income and other material rewards.** Because your good attitude will make you very valuable to other people (your boss, for instance), they, in time, will reward you with money and possessions.

With so much to gain and so little to lose, you might show a good attitude for 30 days. If you don't like it after trying it for 30 days, then go ahead and be as miserable as you want to be. But at least give a positive mental attitude a sincere try.

                                                                    - Steve Simms

## Attitude — These 10 Qualities Make a Winner

Motivational speaker Patrick O'Dooley addresses hundreds of audiences a year. At one point during his speeches, he asks the audience to tell him what words they use to describe "a winner."

He goes to a board or flip chart as people in the audience call out the words they associate with winners and writes down the first ten he hears.

Over the years, O'Dooley has kept a list of these Top 10 Winning Qualities, and he recently compiled them into a list ranked in the order of occurrence:

1. Positive attitude
2. Enthusiastic
3. Determined
4. Motivated
5. Confident
6. Optimistic
7. Dedicated
8. Happy
9. Good listener
10. Patient

This list is useful for what it says, and for what it omits. For example, note that none of these top winning qualities has anything to do with physical or mental ability.

As O'Dooley points out, this indicates that anyone on earth can be a winner because winning is based on attitude, not aptitude. You control whether or not you will be a winner in life, regardless of your natural abilities.

When writing down the list of winning qualities that people call out, O'Dooley invariably misspells one of the words, and someone always points that out to him. Then O'Dooley reveals that he is dyslexic and frequently reversed letters when reading and writing in school. His teachers thought he had low aptitude, so O'Dooley developed what he did have control over, his attitude. He has achieved much more than he ever would have as a perfect speller with a poor attitude.

To make this point another way, he also suggests that his audience imagine some of them are reborn as a five-pound bar of raw iron ore (worth about $5.00) and some are five-pound bars of gold (worth about $30,000). The gold bars begin life worth far more than those made of iron.

But if the gold ore people are complacent, and the iron ore people work on themselves, and transform themselves into watchsprings, for example, they can go from a worth of $5.00 to a worth of hundreds of thousands of dollars — by making the best possible use of what they are.

Although we can't change our "raw materials" much, O'Dooley points out that the "process of refinement is one thing you can control."

- Patrick O'Dooley, *Flight Plan for Living*

## What's The Score

A man stopped to watch a Little League baseball game. He asked one of the youngsters what the score was. "We're behind 18 to nothing," was the answer. "Well," said the man, "I must say you don't look discouraged." "Discouraged?" asked the little boy. "Why should we be discouraged? We haven't come to bat yet."

- *The Best of Bits & Pieces*

## Can Do Attitude

The Italian sculptor Agostino d'Antonio worked diligently on a large piece of marble. Unable to produce his desired masterpiece, he lamented, "I can do nothing with it." Other sculptors also worked this difficult piece of marble, but to no avail.

Michelangelo discovered the sonata and visualized the possibilities in it. His "I can make it happen" attitude resulted in one of the world's masterpieces — *David*.

Experts in Spain concluded that Columbus's plans to discover a new and shorter route to the West Indies was virtually impossible. Queen Isabella and King Ferdinand ignored the report of the experts.

"I can make it happen," Columbus persisted. And he did. Everyone knew the world was flat, but not Columbus. The *Nina*, the *Pinta*, the *Santa Maria*, along with Columbus and his small band of followers, sailed to "impossible" new lands and thriving resources.

The Scotsman George Sweeting was often teased about his hard working attitude and positive life-style. "Scotty, don't you know that Rome wasn't built in a day?" his friends would tease. "Oh, I know," he would answer. "But I wasn't foreman on that job." George Sweeting held the belief, "I can make it happen."

Even the great Thomas Alva Edison discouraged his friend, Henry Ford, from pursuing his fledgling idea of a motorcar. Convinced of the worthlessness of the idea, Edison invited Ford to come and work for him. Ford remained committed and tirelessly pursued his dream. Although his first attempt resulted in a vehicle without reverse gear, Henry Ford knew he could make it happen. And, of course, he did.

"Forget it," the experts advised Madame Curie. They agreed radium was a scientifically impossible idea. However, Marie Curie insisted, "I can make it happen."

Let's not forget our friends Orville and Wilbur Wright. Journalists, friends, armed forces specialists, and even their father laughed at the idea of an airplane. "What a silly and insane way to spend money. Leave flying to the birds," they jeered. "Sorry," the Wright brothers responded. "We have a dream, and we can make it happen." As a result, a place called Kitty Hawk, North Carolina, became the setting for the launching of their "ridiculous" idea.

Finally, as you read these accounts under the magnificent lighting of your environment, consider the plight of Benjamin Franklin. He was admonished to stop the foolish experimenting with lighting. What an absurdity and waste of time! Why, nothing could outdo the fabulous oil lamp. Thank goodness Franklin knew he could make it happen.

You too can make it happen!

*- The Speaker's Sourcebook*

# 4

---

# Making Others Feel Important

*"The greatest compliment anyone can pay you: I
feel good about me whenever I'm around you."*

Francis X. Maguire

Studies have shown that people who feel good about themselves
produce good results, and employees generally treat customers
exactly the way they are treated. So, why don't we make people
feel good? People want to feel important. What this tells us is that
we should do everything we can to improve our interactions with
people and make others feel important, if we are to continue to
nurture their personal career growth. Eighty-five percent of all joy
we get in life comes from interactions with other people. Our
ability to get along with others is directly related to the height of
our own self-esteem, and everything we can do to improve the self-
esteem of others raises our own self-esteem.

## PEOPLE WANT TO FEEL IMPORTANT

Successful corporations and managers in the 2000s will credit their
success to feelings, attitudes, and relationships. As a leader, the
challenge is to be the best you can be and to bring out the best in
others. *It's knowing that employees want to feel important. They
want to be appreciated and cared for, they want information,
and they want a personal relationship with their immediate
supervisors.* Feelings, attitudes, and relationships are, or will be,

the driving force of every truly successful company. It is your attitude, not your aptitude, as my friend and mentor Zig Ziglar says, that is going to bring you success. Attitude is the great difference-maker.

So how can we make these attitudinal adjustments in ourselves, and how do we make others feel important? Remember, your employees want to know "Do you care about me?" You must convey to your employees and customers the message that you truly do care about them as individual contributors.

> You are special when you make other people feel special.
>
> - Rudy Benton

Second, you must communicate with them *a lot*, preferably on an open face-to-face basis. The successful manager spends up to 75% of his/her time communicating. Third, you must remember that you are no longer the boss but the coach, whose main job is creating the workplace environment that will bring out the best in you and in others.

## HOW TO MAKE PEOPLE FEEL IMPORTANT

We can significantly improve our interactions with other people by following these eight recommendations, while continuously remembering that we must be patient in our relationships with others in order to build their trust and respect. Write these down and keep them in a place where you can read and practice them daily.

> The best vitamin for developing friends is B-1.

### Eight Ways to Improve Your People Skills

#### 1.  SMILE

Accept people for who they are. Take the time and effort to learn as much as you can about others before you judge them. Always smile whenever you can. Smiling conveys a thousand words and is the universal symbol of acceptance to others.

## 2. FACE-TO-FACE COMMUNICATIONS

According to IBM, managers should spend up to three-quarters of their time communicating (talking, listening, writing). Face-to-face communication, with opportunities for discussion and questions, is generally preferred. Managers should also learn that employees want the "why" of any policy and procedure change explained.

The most effective way to improve communications is to hold meetings with all your employees on a regular basis. Once employees become convinced that your meetings will be regular and that you will give their suggestions serious attention, they will not be afraid to speak out; and when that occurs, you will know that you are heading on the right track.

## 3. PRAISE

There are three million hungry people in this world, but four million waiting for their first, sincere compliment. Look for the gold in others, not *the dirt*. Be a finder and when you find the good, immediately praise that action. People absolutely love to be told that they are doing well and individually making a positive contribution to the success of their department and/or their company.

Let your employees know when they do well and always praise specific acts and tell them why they are being recognized. This shows caring — important in building trust. It is also important to praise, both verbally and in writing. Words of praise, even if it's a hand-written note, are often kept by employees and referred to for personal reinforcement over long periods of time.

## 4. APPRECIATION

Expressing gratitude is often difficult for most of us. You can simply say "thank you" or write personal notes of appreciation to others. You can also express gratitude in other forms such as treating others as you would guests in your own home and treating them with respect.

We often get everything we want in indirect ways. *If we want a friend, we've got to be a friend; if we want people to be interested in us, we've got to show interest in them.* We will reap what we sow and the best way to become appreciated is to show appreciation and respect to others.

## 5. ADMIRATION

We can show respect and admiration to others by picking out something meaningful, such as their excellent work habits or punctuality, and telling them how much you admire these traits. Or when visiting their home, you can pick out a piece of furniture or lovely picture to admire. On a more personal level, you can admire their tie, or hair or any other item that means a lot to them.

## 6. NEVER CRITICIZE

Destructive criticism undermines the self-esteem of others. It doesn't do any good to tear down the self-esteem of others because, in the process, it tears down your own. Nobody wins unless the criticism is constructive, and it is only constructive when performance is criticized, not the performer. *Remember:* no one ever erected a statue to honor a critic.

## 7. NEVER ARGUE

When you argue, you are telling others they are wrong, and people *hate* being told they are wrong. If you feel that you are being brought into an argument, try to pick out a non-existent third party, like a newspaper or magazine article, and express your point of view by referring to what was said in the newspaper or by another party.

## 8. ATTENTION

People pay attention to what they value. More than anything else, listening is the trait that shows that we care about what others say. The more attention we give by listening patiently and attentively to others, the more appreciation we show for the other person's self-worth.

Three things happen when we listen:

■ It builds trust.
■ It builds character in the listener. It takes a lot of concentration to be a good listener; our mind can clearly understand a person who can speak at a rate of 500 words/minute, whereas most people only talk at 100 words/minute.
■ It builds self-esteem in the speaker.

Some key points in effective listening are to listen attentively, pause before replying, give feedback to achieve clarity in the form of questions, and ask open-ended questions. Listening is a skill that is difficult to master, but is extremely valuable.

The above recommendations should help you get started toward making others feel important. Practice them daily. You will find that people will reciprocate and respond, not react, and that your interactions with others will improve dramatically.

> Kind words can be short and easy to speak, but their echoes are truly endless.
>
> - Mother Teresa

## Lesson in Leadership

If you want to be important, you must make others feel important. What a gift it is to be able to do that! Andrew Carnegie surrounded himself with people who were positive and enthusiastic. One such person was Charles Schwab, the man who was called "Mr. Enthusiasm" and "The Man with the Million Dollar Smile." Charles Schwab knew very little of the steel business but became the first millionaire in his field because of his people skills.

Doing what you're told just won't work anymore and a whole new set of management attitudes and behaviors are required. Are you prepared for these coming changes which are already upon us?

## SUCCESS STORIES

### 99 Ways to say "Very Good"

1. Super good!
2. You've got it made.
3. Super!
4. That's right!
5. That's good.
6. You're really working hard today.
7. You are very good at that.
8. That's coming along nicely.
9. Good work!
10. That's much better!
11. I'm happy to see you working like that.
12. Exactly right.
13. I'm proud of the way you worked today.
14. You are doing much better today.
15. You've just about got it.
16. That's the best you have ever done.
17. You're doing a good job!
18. That's it!
19. Now you've figured it out.
20. That's quite an improvement.
21. Great!
22. I knew you could do it.
23. Congratulations!
24. You're making real progress.
25. Keep working on it, you're improving.
26. Now you have it!
27. You are learning fast.
28. Extraordinary!
29. Couldn't have done it better myself.
30. You are a joy.
31. One more time and you'll have it.
32. You really make my job fun.
33. That's the right way to do it.

34. You're getting better every day.
35. You did it that time!
36. You're on the right track now.
37. Nice going.
38. You haven't missed a thing.
39. Wow!
40. That's the way!
41. Keep up the good work.
42. Terrific!
43. Nothing can stop you now.
44. That's the way to do it!
45. Sensational!
46. You've got your brain in gear today.
47. That's better.
48. That was first class work.
49. Excellent!
50. That's the best ever.
51. You've just about mastered that.
52. Perfect!
53. That's better than ever.
54. Much better!
55. Wonderful!
56. You must have been practicing!
57. You did that very well.
58. Fine!
59. Nice going.
60. You're really going to town.
61. Outstanding!
62. Fantastic!
63. Tremendous!
64. That's how to handle that!
65. Now that's what I call a fine job.
66. That's great.
67. Right on!
68. You're really improving!
69. You're doing beautifully.
70. Superb!
71. Good remembering!

72. You've got that down pat.
73. You certainly did well today.
74. Keep it up!
75. Congratulations — you did it!
76. You did a lot of work today.
77. Well, look at you go!
78. That's it!
79. I'm very proud of you.
80. Marvelous!
81. I like that.
82. Way to go!
83. Now you have the hang of it!
84. You're doing fine.
85. Good thinking.
86. You are really learning a lot.
87. Good going.
88. I've never seen anyone do it better.
89. Keep on trying!
90. You outdid yourself today!
91. Good for you!
92. I think you've got it now.
93. That's wonderful!
94. Good job!
95. You figured that out fast.
96. You remembered!
97. That's really nice.
98. That kind of work makes me happy.
99. It's such a pleasure to work with you.

- Zig Ziglar

## Tell Employees How Important They Are

People leaving their jobs for any number of reasons is no longer a thing of the past. Often it's a better opportunity elsewhere or a fatter paycheck. But, even with the lure of more money, people who are reasonably content with their work and their bosses seldom go out looking for other jobs.

Some supervisors have a higher turnover among their subordinates than others, sometimes embarrassingly so. And often it's the better people who leave. This can be a costly and frustrating problem.

Sometimes, obviously, people have been offered opportunities or salaries that are so extraordinary you couldn't possibly have matched them. All you could have done in any case is let them go and wish them good luck. But don't be too sure. Before you let yourself off the hook, ask yourself a few questions, and answer them as honestly as you can.

- Did I let these people know how important they were to me and to the company? Or did I more or less take them for granted?
- Did I give them a chance to be proud of themselves?
- Did I pass along all the authority I possibly could — or keep them tied to my apron strings?
- Did I give these people — and get for them — the credit and recognition they deserved from me and from others in the company? Or did I tend to leave them in the shadows?
- Was the job a real challenge? Did I do my best to make it so?
- Did I make their work as varied and interesting as possible? Did I show them the possibilities of a promising future? Or did I simply leave them in a rut and *exploit* their abilities to my own advantage?

Don't be too quick to absolve yourself from all blame. If you were responsible, in any respect, it's smarter to realize it than to hide your head in the sand. Unless you change your *attitude* or *actions*, you may lose more than just good people. You may be on the verge of destroying your own company or career as well.

The best time to think of these things, of course, is *before* you lose good people rather than *after.*

*- Personal Excellence*

## Write That Thank-You Note

The key to success, according to management guru Tom Peters, is writing thank you notes. Every time someone does you a favor, or does a good job, sit down and write the person a note. "What about a phone call?" asks Peters. "Good: Do it, but lifting up a phone is pretty easy. Writing a note demonstrates a level of effort and is permanent. Typed or handwritten? Handwritten by a country mile. A two-line, largely unreadable scrawl beats a page and a half on the laser printer."

*- Working Woman*

## Amy's Favorite Doll

One very special Christmas day, little Amy unwrapped a beautiful golden-haired doll given to her by her grand-mother. "It's such a pretty dolly," Amy squealed excit-edly, hugging her new doll. "Oh, thank you, Grandma!"

Amy played with her new doll most of the day, but toward the end of the day, she put down her golden-haired doll and sought out one of her old dolls. Amy cradled the tattered and dilapidated old doll in her arms. Its hair had come off; its nose was broken, one eye was gone, and one arm and a leg were missing.

"Well, well," smiled Grandma. "It looks as though you like that dolly the best."

"I like the beautiful doll you gave me, Grandma," said little Amy. "But I love this old doll the most, because if I didn't love her, no one else would."

*- The Speaker's Sourcebook*

## Acceptance: A Practical Challenge

Dave Galloway shares a heart-rending story about a high-class couple who enjoyed their parties and social eliteness. It was the holiday season, and of course, a festive time for the socialites. Just as they were leaving for one of many parties, the phone rang.

"Hello, Mom," the caller said. "I'm back in the states with an early release from my army duties in Vietnam."

"That's wonderful, son," his mother replied. "When will you be home?"

The young man said, "That all depends. I would like to bring a buddy home with me."

"Sure, bring him home with you for a few days," the mother replied.

"Mother, there is something you need to know about my buddy... both legs have been amputated, one arm is gone, his face is quite disfigured, and one ear and eye are missing. He's not much to look at, but he needs a home real bad."

The mother stammered, "A home? Why don't you bring him along for a few days?"

"You don't understand," the young man pleaded. "I want to bring him home to live."

"I think that is asking a lot, son, but you get home soon so we can spend the holidays together. As for your friend, I'm sorry about his condition, but what would our friends think? How would I explain it to the people at the club? And it would be just too much for your father and..." (The phone went dead.)

Later that night, the couple returned from their party with a message to call the police department in a small California town. The mother placed the call and asked for the chief of police. The man at the other end said, "We have just found a young man with both legs and one arm missing, his face is badly mangled, and one eye and ear are missing. He shot himself in the head. His identification indicates he is your son!"

This "once-upon-a-time" fairy tale does not have a happy ending; and, unfortunately, it is not really a fairy tale. Unconditional acceptance is a reality many people have difficulty comprehending.

How about you? Would you have received the young man with open arms?

*- The Speaker's Sourcebook*

# 5

---

# Managing Confrontation

*"Life is simple until you throw people in it."*

Rich "MR POS" Wilkins

Again, in 1990 Federal Express won the 1st Malcolm Baldrige Quality Award given in the category of Service. Francis X. Maguire, then Senior Vice-President of Federal Express, accepted the award, and in his acceptance speech said that "the successful corporations and managers in the 1990s will credit their success to feelings, attitudes, and relationships." Robert Levering, an author and consultant with the Great Places to Work Institute in San Francisco was recently quoted by *Chief Executive* magazine — "the thing that is going to set you apart from a competitor is a workforce that can cooperate well with each other and with management. Cooperation is especially important in this era of change."

## GETTING ALONG WITH OTHERS

I'm sure that you will agree with me that getting along with our fellow workers and supervisors is very important in creating and maintaining a great workplace, a necessary ingredient to top performance. Life is simple until you throw people in it. As Brian Tracy, a well-known teacher of motivation, says "85% of all joy we get in life comes from positive interactions with other people." It's how we deal with the 15% of our negative interaction with people that will make the difference.

63

The weak can never forgive. Forgiveness is the attribute of the strong.

- Mahatma Gandhi

Some tension and competition in the organization is healthy and inevitable. It keeps all employees on their toes, alert and ready to respond to the next challenge. However, when conflicts become negative, productivity drops, teamwork ceases, and people virtually stop talking to each other. Most people usually react, not respond, to interpersonal attack by either fight or flight.

Controlling anger and criticism in the workplace isn't easy, and leaders who learn to deal with it constructively usually earn trust and respect from both their peers and subordinates. Leaders do earn their authority from below, through trust and respect. Criticism is rampant in America and anger in the workplace is on the increase. Controlling both anger and criticism can and should be taught because they are de-motivators. They can destroy enthusiasm, morale, trust, open communication, values, personal relationships, and affect productivity.

## ASSOCIATE WITH POSITIVE PEOPLE

The success that we will attain is greatly influenced by the people with whom we associate. We have to either "turn around" or get rid of toxic people in the workplace and make it known that

Ego — The disease that afflicts everyone except the carrier.

- John Wooden

"negativity is not welcome here." *I used to think that it was important to associate with positive people and to limit my involvement with negative people. Now I believe that it is essential if you want to be a high achiever and a happy individual, and to develop a great workplace.*

Negative people will make you feel listless, depressed, and drained. Your energy will be drastically affected and your dreams will be mortally wounded. Negative people will wear you down and douse your motivational flame. Do they affect productivity? You can bet on that. Anger is an emotion and always translates into an unwillingness to support the work we are all trying to get accomplished.

In the heat of anger, resentment, or criticism we have a tendency to make wrong, unwise decisions. No matter where you work, there will always be people whose faults and personality defects can be annoying and irritating... *if you let yourself become annoyed and irritated.*

> An apology is a good way to have the last word.

Supervisors, managers, and employees (team members) who let their feelings get out of control in this manner hurt their effectiveness. It also limits their usefulness to the company and might even block their own career advancement.

Keeping a leash on our emotions, or better yet, learning to express our emotions in an appropriate way or "containing" them until we are in an appropriate setting, especially in the world of business, is something we must do ourselves. No one else can do it for us. Everyone gets exasperated once in a while, but if it happens frequently — or if you tend to nurse a grudge afterward — it isn't good and according to Ziglar, you will need a "check up from the neck up to eliminate (or minimize) that stinkin' thinkin'."

## SIX STEPS TO CONTROLLING ANGER AND CRITICISM

So what can you do about it?

1.  You can't control or influence other people sensibly until you first control yourself. That's fundamental. Whenever you start to get irritated, STOP! Grab hold of yourself. Don't get mad. Get curious and try to understand why they are doing what they are doing. Remember, when people anger or criticize you, they aren't necessarily doing it on purpose. To some extent, they can't help acting the way they do because they are products of their environment and past experiences. You might have become just as irritating if you had had the same experience.

So, why be angry? Remember, the minute you get angry you lose, because the action or retaliation you take is not going to be as appropriate as it would have been if you remained calm and open.

Whenever you feel yourself getting angry, try to stop or postpone the discussion and THINK. When you've cooled down a bit, use empathy to see if you could understand the other person's feelings or viewpoint. The more you realize and understand what makes a person act in a certain way, the less irritating it will be. You'll become more tolerant and much more effective. A good technique is to speak softly and call the other person by his/her name.

2.  Change our attitude toward others and accept people for who they are. Take the time and effort to learn as much as you can about them before you judge them. When you do, you will usually see them differently (in a more positive way). And, we always treat people as we see them.

    Always smile whenever you can. It is an absolutely true statement that smiling conveys a thousand words and is the universal symbol of acceptance to others.

3.  Learn to confront people "face-to-face." Communication is 93% body language and it is essential to meet personally and provide plenty of opportunity for discussing whatever ails you or them in a non-threatening manner. This is easier said than done, but it must be done to manage our feelings.

    Our feelings, negative or positive, will affect our attitude and behavior in the workplace. Having a great workplace is becoming widespread in companies. Many companies are even incorporating behavior in their performance evaluations of management.

4.  Look for opportunities to find the gold in others and when you find the good, praise that action. People love to be told that they have done well and are making positive contributions toward the success of their department and their company. This shows caring and is important in defusing anger and criticism, and in building or re-building trust.

Making others feel important will always make you feel important.

5. During the heat of your anger, do not criticize or become argumentative. Criticism is destructive and undermines the self-esteem of others. When you tear down the self-esteem of others, it tears down your own. In positive, caring work environments, people are much less motivated to criticize others. We do become products of our environment.

   When you argue, you are telling people they are wrong and people hate to be told that they are wrong. If you are enticed into an argument, remember to pick out a non-existent third party, like a newspaper, and express your point of view by referring to the article that you have read or heard from another party. This may keep you from getting into trouble.

6. Listen. People pay attention to what they value and listening is the trait that shows that we care about what others say. The more listening we do shows appreciation of the other person's self-worth. The important thing here is that we take the initiative to confront the situation, in order to deal with it.

The above suggestions should help in controlling anger. If you practice these daily you'll find that people will reciprocate and respond positively, not react. You'll also be influencing and motivating others by example. Model the attitudes and behaviors you'd like your employees to emulate and address

> I ask you to judge me by the enemies I have made.
>
> - Franklin D. Roosevelt

conflicts quickly, prior to their growing out of proportion. Incidentally, did you notice the similarity in these recommendations to those used in the previous chapter — making others feel important? Using the six recommendations with everyone will minimize confrontation and develop cooperation and teamwork.

## Lesson in Leadership

Cooperating well with others — interdepartmentally and intradepartmentally — will be another measuring tool for managers in the 21st century. Managers will be interdependent on others in order to be successful. Searching for the right "yes," rather than saying "no" all the time, will become a trait of future leaders, who will depend on cross functional teams.

A recent Korn-Ferry study predicts that within the next decade, companies will have many team leaders rather than single leaders. In order to build winning teams, you must first build winning people. And winning teams require people who cooperate with each other.

Confrontation will never go away — how you handle it is the difference maker. The way I have been successful is quite similar to how I make others feel — important. It is important to confront people immediately in an open, honest, and friendly manner.

## SUCCESS STORIES

### Sweeter Than Revenge

Election campaigns can produce emotional confrontations. In 1755, a twenty-three-year-old colonel was in the midst of a campaign for a seat in the Virginia assembly. Exercising limited judgment, young George Washington made an insulting comment to a hot-tempered young man named Payne. He did not take kindly to the insult and responded by knocking Washington down with a hickory stick. Soldiers rushed to Washington's assistance, but he called them off, got to his feet, and exited from the scene.

Early the next morning, Washington wrote Payne a letter requesting that they meet at a tavern. Payne obliged, wondering what motives and demands Washington would have. He was sure an apology or even a duel might be requested. However, Washington met Payne with an apology for his derogatory remarks, requested forgiveness, and offered his hand in peace.

That may be called politically expedient, but Washington considered it personally necessary to ensure internal peace.

*- The Speaker's Sourcebook*

## It Could Have Been Worse

Understanding, willingness to accept failure, and sincere appreciation were a few of the qualities contributing to John D. Rockefeller's success. It was reported that when one of his partners, Edward T. Bedford, failed miserably and ended up losing the company a million dollars, Rockefeller responded with a classic statement. He didn't criticize Bedford because he knew he had done his best. However, he did call him into the office and said, "I think it is honorable that you were able to salvage 60% of the money you invested in the South America venture. That's not bad; it's splendid. We don't always do as well as that upstairs."

*- The Speaker's Sourcebook*

## Arguing Over Trivialities

A loaf of bread fell from a bakery truck. As it hit the pavement, a crumb broke off. Three sparrows swooped down on the crumb and began fighting over it. One bird finally succeeded in flying off with the crumb, the two others in close pursuit. A series of frenzied aerial maneuvers followed until the crumb was at last consumed by one of the birds.

The loaf of bread was untouched. Only the crumb had seemed worth the fight. If the birds had displayed more vision and less greed, they could have all been satisfied.

People, like birds, quarrel over trivialities. In the heat of the struggle life's bigger, more enriching prizes escape them.

*- Bits & Pieces*, Economics Press, Fairfield, NJ

## 12 Ways To Criticize Effectively

Here are 12 guidelines to remember the next time you have to tell someone that he or she has done something wrong:

- Identify the behavior that you want to criticize. Direct your criticism at action, not the person.
- Make criticisms specific. Not, "You always miss deadlines;" but, "You missed the March 15 deadline for your report."
- Be sure the behavior you're criticizing can be changed. Foreign accents, baldness, and other things tangentially related to some business dealings cannot always be changed.
- Use "I" and "We" to stress that you want to work out the problem together, rather than making threats.
- Make sure the other person understands the reason for your criticism.
- Don't belabor the point. Short and sweet; no lectures.
- Offer incentives for changed behavior. Offer to help the person correct the problem.
- Don't set a tone of anger or sarcasm. Both are counterproductive.
- Show the person you understand his or her feelings.

■ If you're putting your criticism in writing, cool off before writing the critical letter or memo. Be sure only the person it is intended for sees it.
■ Start off by saying something good.

At the end, reaffirm your support and confidence in the person.

- Highlights, *Blue Cross and Blue Shield*

# 6

---

# Leading Change

*"Today, more than ever, the successful manager must be a change seeker — always having a constructive discontent with existing practices. An organization without change seekers will become rigid and atrophied."*

Lou Boland (circa 1965)

Price Pritchett says that high-velocity change in business has become real and more of it is expected, and at a faster pace. The only question is whether we're going to be able to ride the wave of change or be beached by it. Either we change or we'll get changed.

As leaders, we are expected to *lead* change. The question today, in most major companies is, "How can we help our people accept that we must change?" Companies will be successful and employees will accept and be responsive to change *if* they can produce a long-term voluntary change in the attitude and behavior of management and employees. The opportunity is nowhere — NO WHERE or NOW HERE? The choice is yours.

Successful companies help people appreciate the need to deal positively with change and create a workplace environment where people willingly desire to move in a constructive direction, because they want to and feel that it is the right thing to do. They've learned that it is difficult to unlearn behavior and change. *Managers must lead by example, model the new behaviors, and first "buy in" and be involved. Then they can lead change in the organization.*

## HERE'S WHAT SOME LEADING CEOs
## AND ORGANIZATIONS SAY ABOUT CHANGE

The first thing that happens when people become aware of an upcoming change is, they stop working. The rumor mill starts to heat up and employees begin to experience fear for their continued employment. You see an increase in anger and hostility. The feeling is that while they have been loyal to the organization, the organization is no longer loyal to them. The employee who does not have the personal resources to deal with the emotional pressure may experience problems at home or with work relationships.

- Dan Evans, Personnel Manager,
Xerox Corporation

Some people really become scared when change occurs. Maybe they shouldn't, but they do. You have to be able to relate to that and say to yourself, "I have to be tolerant of that and I have to assuage it, and channel it constructively."

- Michael Blumenthal, former CEO,
Unisys

Change has considerable psychological impact on the human mind. To the fearful, it is threatening because it means that things may get worse. To the hopeful, it is encouraging because things may get better. To the confident, it is inspiring because the challenge exists to make things better. Obviously, then, one's character and frame of mind determine how readily he brings about change and how he reacts to change that is imposed on him.

- King Whitney, Jr.,
Personnel Laboratory, Inc.

Our culture has a lot of denial concerning the human pain associated with significant loss. If a parent dies, for example, you are expected to be back to work in a few days, and back to "normal" in a few months. Being laid off after many years of steady employment can be like an unexpected death or divorce.

> \- Earl Hipp,
> Health Action

A poll of senior managers at down-sized companies by Right Associates found that 74% believed employees had lower morale, feared future cutbacks, and distrusted management.

Future shock is the shattering stress and disorientation that we induce in individuals by subjecting them to too much change in too short a time.

> \- Alvin Toffler, *Future Shock*

A survey of 1,468 restructured companies by the Society for Human Resource Management reports that employee productivity either stayed the same or worsened after layoffs.

Over the years, the relentless pressure of cost cutting had created with Heinz a mounting feeling of bile. There was an ever-increasing feeling of hostility among the employees. Layoffs create a degree of insecurity because workers wonder if 50 people were cut last year and 100 cut this year, how many will go next year?

> \- Anthony J.F. O'Reilly, Chairman and CEO,
> Heinz Inc.

There was no warning or explanation for the cutbacks, but each time they assured us that this was the last time around. I learned more from the gossip going around than from anything the company told us. My feelings about the company have changed: I don't feel the company is being up-front with us. Everyone in my department is ready to jump to another company.

> \- Employee of a Fortune 500 company

We believe that we have to manage for the longer term, protect our people from cyclical, changing markets, and if they know we're going to do that, they will help us solve the problem. When external realities create changes in the market... your obligation is to find a way to retrain and redeploy those employees, rather than saying, "Oops, the markets changed. Too bad, gang, you're fired."

- Irvine O. Hockaday, Jr., Chairman and CEO,
Hallmark Cards

You have to help people appreciate the need to deal constructively with the changing environment. If we're doing our job, we need to understand the rapidity and magnitude of the changes taking place and provide people with all the tools we can to cope with change.

- Robert Haas, Chairman and CEO,
Levi Strauss & Co.

If there is anything I really picked up on, it was making sure that gobs of written communication went out and that good people were in charge of that. I also personally did a lot of traveling in that period. One must not under-rate the importance of a personal appearance of some-one who has become a symbol of the change.

- Michael Blumenthal, former CEO,
Unisys

We don't want people to come to us as a marriage. We want them to think of it as dating. Don't come here for security, come here for excitement.

- Human Resources Manager,
American Federal Savings Bank

*Inform employees why reengineering is necessary. Tell them where the organization is headed.* This way they'll be more likely to get on board.

*Announce reengineering with a brief (one page) statement.* An effective technique is to hypothesize what would happen if the company chose to do nothing.

*During reengineering, communicate weekly.* A video broadcast, newsletter, or talk by the CEO all can be effective.

*Lay out the facts.* Be honest — even if reengineering means the company will learn to do dramatically more with what will look like fewer people. The truth is far better than building cynicism in the organization.

> \- James Champy, co-author
> of *Reengineering the Corporation*

Many of us are being dragged kicking and screaming into this new technology because we're used to hardware, not software — but success will depend on how well we handle people.

> \- Richard F. Teerlink, Chief Executive
> of Harley-Davidson

There is little question that we have a lot to learn about living with change, and thriving in an ever-changing environment. Most of us have been brought up to fear change because change takes us out of or away from our comfort zone and we naturally respond negatively. Our general reaction

**In order for a goal to be effective, it must effect change.**

is heavy resistance, and consequently people stop working and the number one thing on our minds is, "How will this change affect me?"

Effective training programs on leading change take the following factors into consideration:

■ You can't train anyone to do anything that he or she doesn't fundamentally believe in.

■ Employees should be allowed to reflect on values and align personal values with company values.

■ "Buy in" is absolutely essential and some employees just won't be able to accept change and should be let go.

As an agent for change, you need to recognize the employees' fear of change and take on these roles:

■ catalyst
■ visionary
■ spokesperson
■ empathic listener
■ problem-solver
■ negotiator

■ resource provider
■ coach and cheerleader
■ stabilizer
■ maintenance person
■ and most important, have a positive attitude.

## CREATING AN ENVIRONMENT FOR CREATIVITY AND CHANGE ACCEPTANCE

Keeping these roles in mind, you can provide the training and create an environment for creativity and "change-acceptance," if you follow these seven steps:

### 1. Develop trust.
Give employees a lot of information and reasons why things are happening differently and how they will affect the company, them (as a group) and each individual. Copers need to be communicated with a lot, and mostly face-to-face, in order to retain their sense of control and ability to trust. Keep in mind that it takes time to develop trust and patience and it is essential for the change process to work.

## 2. Remember how people respond to change.

The number one question is, "How will this affect me?" It's important to answer that question quickly and as honestly as you can. Bruce Johnson of International Living Communication says, "only 12% of our working population are innovators or early adopters; 60% are mid-adopters who with proper training could learn to use change to their benefit; and 28% will have real difficulty without excellent training and leadership."

Ask employees for their input and act on their input (in a timely manner). It's important to get employees involved, and to help them express their ideas. It is important that they experience success early on and celebrate small wins. Every new idea goes through three stages:

1. It won't work
2. It costs too much
3. I knew it was great all along

You can by showing support for their ideas and help them overcome the negativity stages that many people associate with new ideas and change. A real problem in America is that management is perceived as tearing people down, rather than building them up. Look at the employee suggestion system, which for many years has been an employee rejection system.

In the U.S. only 0.1% of employees offer suggestions and only 25% of the suggestions are implemented (*The Corporate Coach* by Jim Miller). Employees don't participate because they are not only not encouraged, they are discouraged. Once a suggestion is submitted, most reviewers don't get back to the suggestor for months, and then with criticism. This says clearly to the employees — **I don't care.**

The word "suggestion" implies that workers can only suggest and that they aren't sufficiently educated, intelligent, or responsible enough to make decisions. Don't you agree that the negative word — suggestion — should never again be used? Let's get it out of our vocabulary and replace it with something more positive such as improvement system.

In 48 BC, Confucius said:

**Tell people something and they forget
Show them and they'll remember.
*Involve* them and they'll understand.**

### 3. Make the change personally first.
Once you have bought in on the change, you could then logically ask for support from others.

### 4. Show employees how the change will benefit them.
No matter how worthy the change might be in your eyes, it is unlikely to be supported by others — given a natural resistance to change — unless you can make the advantages obvious in *their* eyes. Focus on finding out what others' needs are and how the change you want to introduce will meet those needs. Keeping changes simple, divisible, and even reversible will help gain support. Copers will feel reassured if they can learn something new, get a raise, do their jobs easier, or see other benefits in the situation.

### 5. Train.
When employees haven't been exposed to new technology — for instance, having a seemingly complicated computer system arrive on their desk — it can be frightening and job-threatening to them. But if they've been coached through the process in an environment where it's OK to make mistakes, once trained, they will wind up as the biggest champions of the new technology, and influence others.

### 6. Encourage influencers to influence others.
Once identifying your influencers (i.e., those employees who have bought in), encourage them to be your helpers. Because people have a high need to control, they can become great team leaders and training assistants.

### 7. Be patient with the process.
People need time to change their behavior. Treat each individual according to their personal needs and you'll be pleased with the results.

## Changing the Way We Think

| Issues | From | To |
|---|---|---|
| Mistakes | Who | Why |
| Defects | Fix | Prevent |
| Errors | Inevitable | Not accepted |
| Performance | Cost/Schedule | Customer requirements |
| Training | Cost | Investment |
| Measurement | Justify | Define problems |
| Vendor choice | Price | Price/Value |
| Change | Resisted | Way of Life |
| Technology | Automate | Empower |
| Information flow | Vertical | Horizontal/Vertical |
| Management style | Enforcer | Coach |
| Non-Management | Do | Plan/Think/Do |
| Performance goal | Standard | Better than yesterday |

To make change happen, you need to have a positive attitude, provide training that is employee-centered (people skills), first "buy-in" on the change, keep others informed, and encourage employees to be involved.

## Lesson in Leadership

Realize that one of your employees' greatest fears is change. Leaders are expected to lead the change process and help employees overcome their fears. With your encouragement in a positive, caring, and change-accepting environment, given proper training, employees will begin to respond (not react) in a positive manner.

Only 12% of employees are innovators or early adapters to change. The others need to be nurtured and involved in the process to buy-in and be productive in a changing world.

## SUCCESS STORIES

### How Wrong You Were, Mr. Wright!

In 1870, a short-sighted bishop expressed to the president of a small denominational college his firm biblical conviction that nothing new could be invented. The educator responded in disagreement and believed there was much yet to be discovered.

"Why, I believe it may even be possible for men in the future to fly through the air like birds," the college professor said.

The bishop was taken aback. "Flying is reserved for the angels," he insisted. "I beg you not to mention that again lest you be guilty of blasphemy!"

That mistaken bishop was none other than Milton Wright, the father of Orville and Wilbur. Only thirty-three years later, his two sons made their first flight in a heavier-than-air machine, which was the forerunner of the airplane. How wrong you were, Mr. Wright!

*- The Speaker's Sourcebook*

### The Fear of Change

Some changes are hard to accept. In 1829 Martin Van Buren, then the governor of New York, wrote this to the President.

"The canal system of this country is being threatened by the spread of a new form of transportation known as 'railroads'....as you may well know, railroad carriages are pulled at the enormous speed of 15 miles per hour by engines, which, in addition to endangering life and limb of passengers, roar and snort their way through the countryside. The Almighty certainly never intended that people should travel at such breakneck speed."

- Sylvia Simmons,
*How to be the Life of the Podium*, AMA

## Be Innovative

Phil Romano, the founder of Fuddruckers, a national hamburger chain, once owned a small out-of-the-way Italian restaurant called Macaroni's. He packed the place on Monday and Tuesday nights — a time when most restaurants struggle to keep their doors open. Here's why. Apart from the obvious fact that Macaroni's served good food, Romano had a gimmick backed on an old Psych 101 principle — random rewards beget regular behavior. In this case, the behavior was eating at Macaroni's on an off-night.

If you happened to be dining there on a randomly chosen Monday or Tuesday night, you and the other 200 or so customers received a letter instead of a bill at the end of the meal. The letter stated that because Macaroni's mission was to make people feel like guests, it seemed awkward to charge guests for having a good time. So, once each month on a Monday or Tuesday night — and always unannounced — everyone would eat free.

Here's what the stunt cost Romano. One night 'comped' out of 30 reduced his revenues by 3.3%. But he had a full house on eight nights a month when the place would normally be empty. And word-of-mouth testimonials are one of the most effective forms of advertising.

In one fell swoop, Romano got a couple of a hundred tongues wagging, "You won't believe what happened to us last night...!"

T. Scott Gross,
*Positively Outrageous Service*

# 7

---

# Motivating Employees for Higher Productivity

*"Management is nothing more than motivating people."*

Lee Iacocca

It is amazing what people will do if they feel valuable in their organization. Your success as a leader will be determined by your ability to elicit extraordinary performance from people, and by your ability to build a winning team by motivating others, through coaching and leading by example, to give their very best toward the achievement of the goals of the organization. You can be successful if you make people feel good about themselves and others.

If people feel good about themselves, they will be motivated to solve problems and they will be excited about their work, so they will look for ways to get things done without being watched and prodded. They will *respond* to situations rather than react. When we react, we are controlled by the situation. When we respond, we are able to seek positive solutions without blaming others or feeling negative. When we respond, we come from a position of caring and respect.

The following excerpts are from *Chief Executive* magazine in its July 1996 edition entitled "The People/Performance Paradox":

- "Many companies say that their people are their greatest asset. But do they really believe it or more importantly, do they act as if they believe it?"

- "Executives are beginning to look for ways to tap into the human potential, exploring new methods of managing, motivating and redefining the fundamental relationship between employee and the company; treating employees as appreciating assets that increase in value over time."

- "Corporations need to cultivate a core of longer-term, skilled, motivated employees. Those who will be our leaders in the 21st century must understand that people-embedded skills will be critical to their success — not financial resources and physical assets."

- "There is a real correlation between being a great place to work and overall success." A great workplace is one "where you trust the people you work for, have pride in what you do, and enjoy the people you work for."

- "People can provide the best in customer service only if they know what it feels like to be first in the eyes of the employer. *The growth of a company is based on the growth of individuals and growth motivation can increase productivity by 10, 20, and even 100%.*"

## THE THREE R'S OF MANAGEMENT

Let's focus on the Three R's of Management — *recognition and appreciation, rewards, and reinforcement (encouragement)*. You've heard and read a lot about quality in the 1990s and perhaps you're tired of hearing about it. Quality, like change, is here to stay. What is quality? Some people think their company is a quality company, but if your company is not ensuring that employees are happy, quality is only skin deep. You see, employees treat their customers exactly the same as they are treated. Goethe once said, "*If you treat an individual as he is, he will stay as he is, but if you treat him as if he were*

---

The most important thing about goals is having them.

- Geoffrey F. Abert

---

*what he ought to be and could be, he will become what he ought to be and could be."* Make people feel special and important, help them achieve what they

> **M**orale is the essence of achievement.

want and conquer their fears, and you will be more likely to develop motivated, winning teams.

Winning teams are comprised of individuals who are willing and able to be on a team and contribute their special talents toward a common goal. They possess the following characteristics:

- No one is on a pedestal; every job is important.
- Even the superstars do better if they focus on teamwork.
- Everyone participates and every player counts.
- Every team player focuses on the goal.
- If one person fails, the team fails (never let a teammate fail).
- Teams make average people great and great people humble.
- On teams, people are empowered.
- Individuals put their ego below the ego of the team. The team becomes the hero and credit goes to the team.
- Success as a team gets individuals recognized.

## TEN STEPS IN MOTIVATING OTHERS

Here are ten ideas that you can use to motivate others and develop winning teams:

1. **Selecting the right people for the job.** Your ability to hire and/or select the right people on teams is important. You should hire as much for attitude as you do for aptitude. Take your time in hiring and have the courage to get rid of the difficult people in your organization who are toxic and demotivate others.

   Equally important to understand is that you often have to play with the hand you're dealt (the only thing that you have that the competition doesn't is *your* people) and values-training courses such as Zig Ziglar's "Strategies for Success," should be compulsory training programs for the employees who were with the organization when you arrived. With proper leadership and training, most people can and will change over time.

2. **Keep jobs challenging and interesting.** Challenging work is the number one requirement for job satisfaction and close behind is interesting work. Nothing demotivates people faster than lack of a challenge.

3. **Communicate your expectations.** A major reason for demotivation is "not knowing what's expected of you." People need clear goals and high standards in order to feel like the winners they were born to be. Demand excellence from yourself and from others and stop accepting mediocrity.

4. **Involve the employee.** Pride of ownership is a most compelling motivator. Share the "big picture" as to why employees are asked to do what they are doing and how their work benefits others and always invite employees to offer their opinion and become active participants.

5. **Manage by exception.** Wherever possible, stay clear of the tasks assigned, other than to continue to encourage and coach the employee. Require mutually agreed upon objectives only, such as reporting on a scheduled basis.

6. **Provide sufficient training.** The average company spends only 1% of its operating costs on training, which yields an average ROI of 30 to 1 in improved performance and profitability. Does that make sense to you? It doesn't make sense to me. Investing in training that meets the specific needs of each individual will always increase productivity.

7. **Mentor your employees.** Individual attention by a senior staff member is a major motivator of peak performance, builds self-esteem, improves self-image of the employee, and builds self confidence, all antecedents to success. Mentoring requires a strong commitment and genuine caring.

8. **Lead by example.** Become the kind of leader your employees will admire and respect, i.e., one who "walks the talk" and will listen to staff and follow-up on promises.

9. **Treat employees well.** Be considerate, kind, caring and courteous. Treat each employee as if they were your friend, partner or client and they will respond in kind.

10. **Continuously practice the 3 R's of management.** Regularly show your appreciation and recognize staff members for a job well done. Whatever method you use, take it to heart. It costs very little and pays huge dividends. There is nothing more important than making your staff members feel important and when you consistently look for the gold in them, you'll find some in yourself.

Motivating yourself and others isn't easy. You've got to work on it daily because motivation doesn't last. Brian Tracy, a well-known motivational speaker and trainer, suggests that we motivate ourselves daily by using the following techniques:

- Dream big dreams.
- Do what you love to do.
- Focus on your unique talents and abilities.
- Accept 100% responsibility.
- Develop a clear sense of direction.
- Never consider the possibility of failure.
- Dedicate yourself to continuous improvement.
- Develop a workaholic mentality.
- Get around the right people.
- Be teachable.
- Be prepared to climb peak to peak.
- Develop resilience and always bounce back.
- Unlock your inborn creativity.
- Be an unshakable optimist.
- Dedicate yourself to serving.
- Develop a reputation for speed and dependability.
- Be impeccably honest.
- Concentrate single-mindedly on one thing at a time.
- Be decisive.
- Be self-disciplined.
- Back everything with persistence and determination.

You are able to motivate others only by example. When you understand how powerful motivation is to getting things done and achieving top performance and one's potential, it is an awesome skill to have. All high achievers have positive attitudes and possess the skill of being able to motivate themselves and others.

> **P**eople with goals succeed because they know where they're going.
> - Earl Nightingale

Motivation is knowing what it is you enjoy or value — and doing it. Everyone is unique and great leaders take the time to get to know their employees and what motivates them. So, how do leaders motivate others? Here are some ways:

## EIGHT WAYS TO INCREASE PRODUCTIVITY

### I. Motivate Yourself First

Let's take a closer look at Brian Tracy's 21 Steps to Self-Motivation. Before you can motivate others, you first must motivate yourself and set the example by "walking the talk."

1.  **Dream Big Dreams.** Dreams are powerful motivators and I look upon them as goals on wings. All successful people and leaders have goals and dreams. Let me give you some examples:

    ■ Tom Watson named his very small company, which operated out of a garage, International Business Machines. What vision!

    ■ Henry Ford had a vision of creating the V-8 engine, and at one time was even advised by his good friend Thomas Edison that he should give up on the idea and go on to other things. But Ford persisted.

    ■ Thomas Edison had 10,000 failures before he invented the electric lamp and 50,000 failures prior to his discovery of the storage battery. He looked upon each failure as a step toward accomplishing his dream.

- Walt Disney was a failure (in other people's eyes, not his) as an artist and went bankrupt twice before Disneyland and Disney World became a reality. He never stopped dreaming.
- Martin Luther King surely had a dream.
- It's been said that Lee Iacocca used to doodle as a youngster and filled out his last name as follows:

> **I**
> **A**m
> **C**hairman
> **O**f
> **C**hrysler
> **C**orporation of
> **A**merica.

- Harvey Wertlieb, a personal friend of mine, is not well known. In 1990, he owned one nursing home outside of Washington, DC. He changed the name of his company to Global Health Management, which also changed his direction by expanding his horizons. By 1996, he owned ten nursing homes and employed over 1,200 employees. Part of his dream was to purchase poorly-run nursing homes and change their image, which he accomplished. In the past two years, his firm has been acquired twice and he is now part of the #1 company in the nursing home industry. Very few people know Harvey Wertlieb, but he's achieved his success in the same manner as the well-known people I used as examples, using the same leadership principles they did.

2. **Do What You Love To Do.** It's motivating and exciting when you love what you do. The top 10% in their field are doing what they love to do. How do we know if we love what we do? Some indicators of love, or passion, include: can't wait to get to work; not criticizing; doing the job right the first time; receiving commendations from those we serve — our customers, both internal and external; being on time every day and not missing work; helping one another to get the job done; meeting safety standards; and being involved.

3. **Focus on Your Unique Talents and Abilities.** A person's talent is their *behavior*, including traits of assertiveness, discernment (common sense), ability to relate to others, self-confidence and positive self-image, intensity, and values (especially honesty, trustworthy, responsibility, and ethical). This is what constitutes uniqueness. *There have been over 15 billion people who have walked this earth and only one you.*

4. **Be Responsible and Accept Responsibility.** Don't blame others or offer excuses. View yourself as self-employed. When you accept that notion, you'll go from being reactive to proactive.

5. **Set and Achieve Goals.** The master skill is the ability to set goals for every part of your day. Only 3% of the professional workforce have goals and studies indicated that these 3% of the study group, who set goals, will achieve more than the 97% who had not. Also, a recent UCLA study showed that people with goals training earn over $7,400/month, while people without this training are earning $3,400/month. Clear and written goals are like having your hands on the wheel. Do you have control over where you're going and if you don't know where you are going, how are you going to get there?

6. **Never Consider the Possibility of Failure.** Robert Schuler says that the only failure in life is not trying. Try, try, try. Failure is the *foundation* of success. Most people will say failure is the opposite of success — "conformance to the status quo" is. We've got to fail in order to succeed. Babies crawl and fall down before learning to walk. Kids fall down before learning to ride a bike. Adults also make mistakes and it's okay to make mistakes as long as you learn from them. All successful people in life have failed and many have failed many times. Tom Watson of IBM once told his employees to double their failure rate and they would learn much more, at a quicker pace. Mr. Watson also knew that for every thing his employees did wrong, they did twelve things right. What a great leader he was. According to Steve Brown, *"Everything worth doing is worth doing poorly, until you can do it right."*

7. **Dedicate Yourself to Continuous Development, both Personally and Professionally.** The future belongs to the competent and you should follow the 3% Rule, which is to invest 3% of your income back into yourself each year. To earn more, you must learn more. Become a continuous learner. Continue your professional education and do the following — read 60 minutes/day in your field of expertise, attend 1 seminar every three months, listen to motivational audio cassettes in your car, and subscribe to *Readers Digest*. In particular, read their "Word Power" column and learn twenty new words per week. That will do wonders for your vocabulary.

8. **Develop a Workaholic Mentality.** Work hard, hard, hard and work all the time you work. Most people do not and are less than 50% effective because of their socializing and conducting personal business while at work.

   The only time success comes before work is in the dictionary. Leaders will tell you that. They work 50 plus hours/week and often, on weekends. Do more than what you are paid to do and you'll eventually be paid for what you do.

9. **Associate With the Right People.** Identify with a reference group that is goal-oriented, action-oriented and service-oriented. Avoid negative, toxic people and use nourishing winners as your "benchmark." Nourishing people are positive and supportive. They lift your spirits and are a joy to be around. Negative people will drag you to their level and "condition" you. Les Brown refers to them as "Dream Killers." The success you attain will be greatly influenced by the people with whom you associate. So, surround yourself with positive, inspirational people who will encourage you and mentor you.

10. **Be Teachable.** Be open to new information and be willing to change your mind. In order to do that, you've got to change the input in your mind. Ninety percent of the input we hear daily is negative and we've got to consciously replace the negativity with the positive. Read Horatio Alger stories and listen to motivational tapes. U.S. astronauts do, as well as all successful people.

11. **Be Prepared to Climb Peak to Peak.** Develop a long-term perspective and don't get caught in the moment. All of life is cyclical and you should know that you will experience lows and highs. Don't be influenced by the lows.

12. **Develop Resilience and Bounce Back Always and Quickly.** Disappointment is unavoidable and a natural part of life. The only thing you can do is bounce back. General Patton once described success as one's ability to *always bounce back quickly and as high as you can.* He said, "Everyone experiences set backs and as long as you could lift a finger, get off the ground as quickly as you could." *Get the bounce.* Be unstoppable.

13. **Unleash Your Inborn Creativity.** Zig Ziglar says that we are born to win and conditioned to lose. You are a genius. As long as you're clear about what you want to do and where you want to go, you'll begin to find solutions to solve your problems. Our gift from God is life; how we live our life is our gift back to Him. Too many people make a living rather than make a life. John Wooden describes success as the peace of mind which is a direct result of self-satisfaction in knowing that you did your best to become the best that you are capable of becoming, using the abilities you have.

14. **Be An Optimist.** Be a positive, enthusiastic person, looking for the good in every situation. Look for the best in others and it will pump people up.

    In 1908, Andrew Carnegie was the richest man in the country and America's first billionaire. It was said that he attained this remarkable position not by being more brilliant and talented than anyone else, but by having an instinct for finding brilliant, talented people and surrounding himself with them. He once had 43 millionaires working for him. When asked by reporters where he found these millionaires, he answered, "These employees were not rich when they came here. You develop people in the same manner as you mine gold. You have to remove tons of dirt before finding a single ounce of gold. But you don't go in there looking for the dirt, you go in looking for the gold."

    What an important lesson to learn — if we only would.

15. **Dedicate Yourself to Serving Others.** Zig Ziglar's training programs all share a common theme: *"You can have everything in life you want, if you will just help enough other people get what they want."*

    Service to others makes a difference and results in rewards and has meaning and purpose. You'll feel wonderful about yourself and make many friends along the way, who will help you in life. Successful people serve others.

16. **Develop a Reputation for Speed and Dependability.** Less than 2% of people have a bias for action. People who have a sense of urgency about them and are dependable become difference-makers. DO IT NOW.

17. **Be Impeccably Honest With Yourself and Others.** Honesty was the most-named trait of successful leaders in a recent study. Steve Brown is credited with saying, *"Anyone who thinks that they can stay at the top who is not honest is dumb."* Be true to yourself and to others. *Never compromise your integrity and set "peace of mind" as your highest goal.* Consistency with this highest principle will also generate tremendous self-confidence.

18. **Concentrate Single-mindedly on One Thing at a Time.** This is a mark of successful leaders. Finish what you start. All achievement depends on it. The more you do this, the more successful you will be.

19. **Be Decisive.** Get serious about success. The #1 reason why people aren't successful is that they haven't yet decided to be. Stop whining and start winning — be the winner you were born to be.

20. **Be Self-disciplined.** Self-discipline is self-mastering, self-control, and persistence in action. The #1 determinant of character is the ability to **follow-through.** Follow-up is another trait commonly found in successful people.

21. **Back Everything with Persistence and Determination.** Unless you want something badly, you're unlikely to get what you want. If you are persistent and determined, 95% of your goals will be achieved.

Do these things and you will motivate others by your example and achieve the success in life that you've set for yourself as a goal.

## II. Know Your Employees

Take the time to get to know your employees and treat them well. People treat others in the same way that they themselves are treated. Remember, people are motivated for different reasons.

Employees think differently than their supervisors. Supervisors think employees are mostly motivated by money; employees say that they want appreciation more than anything else. The following is a list of what employees *want* most, and a list of what supervisors *think* they want.

### Knowing Your Employees

| Employees | Supervisors |
| --- | --- |
| Appreciation | Good wages |
| Feeling "in" on things | Job security |
| Understanding attitude | Promotion opportunities |
| Job security | Good working conditions |
| Good wages | Interesting work |
| Interesting work | Loyalty from management |
| Promotion opportunities | Tactful discipline |
| Loyalty from management | Appreciation |
| Good working conditions | Understanding attitude |
| Tactful discipline | Feeling "in" on things |

*The Working Communicator*

*What employees want most and what supervisors think they want can be two completely different things.*

## III. Reduce the Demotivators

Help people get what they want and help them overcome their fears through encouragement. People are motivated most by recognition and appreciation, feeling important and involved, and interesting, challenging work. They fear failure, rejection, change, public speaking, confrontation, and sometimes even success. The leader's job is to help employees overcome these fears.

## IV. Listen With Empathy

Listen both physically and reflectively. People feel good because their leader listened to them. People feel hurt when the leader doesn't listen.

## V. Build Their Self-Esteem Through Affirmation

Don't criticize, condemn, or complain. Look for the gold in others. Make them feel important and make your praise specific, immediate, written, and in public.

## VI. Expect the Best

Raise your expectations and communicate your expectations through affirmations. If you want the best out of a person, you must always look for their best. Don't accept mediocrity.

## VII. Build Your Relationship

Communicate your commitment to them. Show you care. Accept them unconditionally. Trust is the glue in any relationship and it only comes when people care and communicate a lot — verbally, if possible.

## VIII. Be a Smart People Manager

People must know *what is important, why it's important and why they're important.* Answer the "what's in it for me?" questions. Show them how they can make a difference. Provide the right resources and the proper environment. Provide constant, positive performance feedback. Harness the power of the entire group. Enlist them to set performance standards. Help them see the benefits over the cost. Provide them with appropriate freedom and structure. Involve them in the decision process. Keep them informed. Communicate regularly and have fun together.

*A great company is one where profits are not something to be achieved at the expense of the people responsible for creating them.* It is amazing what people will do if they work in a positive, caring environment with an inspirational leader who is honest, competent and shares his or her vision.

---

## Lesson in Leadership

Leaders motivate by example, and that is one of the best ways to motivate others. Praising, recognizing and rewarding employees no longer will be optional in managing people. It is vital that you motivate your people. Companies will continually try to do more with fewer employees and motivation is the key to individual and team achievement. It lets the employee know that they are important and their work is appreciated.

Remember that motivating yourself and others isn't easy and you've got to work on it daily, because motivation doesn't last. I use symbols and slogans to help me stay motivated. I wear lapel pins that say "Attitude," "110%," "I care," and a "bee" which helps me model what I expect of myself. The bee is a symbol for me for "bee-ing the best I can be." I post slogans such as "Attitude makes the difference," "10% more than the year before," "Put the Care back into service," and I keep thank-you notes and "I like notes" within sight at all times to remind me how important motivation really is. Motivation takes a lot of time, effort, and follow-up, but it's worth it. Nothing works better at bringing out the best in others and isn't that the goal of leadership? The bee also represents "intelligent ignorance." Everyone knows that the bee's body is too heavy for its wings and, technically, it shouldn't fly. However, no one told the bee, so the bee flies. Embed that thought in your mind so it'll be easy to always remember it. There is no "t" in "can."

## SUCCESS STORIES

### Harness The Power Of Recognition

In 1963, Mary Kay sold $198,000 in cosmetics. By 1993, sales were more than $600 million, and the Mary Kay sales force had topped 300,000. Each summer, more than 30,000 Mary Kay beauty consultants travel to Dallas and pay to attend a seminar — three days of nonstop recognition with minks, diamonds, color-coded suits, sashes, badges, crowns, emblems, flowers, jewelry, kisses, hugs, hand holding, tears, and stories of amazing success. Salespeople come to the seminar for recognition, and it's recognition they get.

Those who think this works for Mary Kay housewives but has little to do with the world of business are way off the mark. Two-thirds of these beauty consultants have full-time jobs in addition to selling Mary Kay. Several are lawyers. There are pediatricians, and even a Harvard MBA.

When considering the issue of when the Mary Kay reward-by-recognition practice will become mainstream, John Kotter, the Knonosoke Matsushita Professor of Leadership at Harvard Business school, says "The genius of great leaders is that they understood money is only one of the things that make people light up." Applause, prizes, and peer recognition are very powerful. Mary Kay Ash is way ahead of the rest of us. Cash is a secondary benefit — *recognition* is the emotional compensation that brings the enthusiasm that creates success.

- The Genesis Enterprise:
Creating Peak-to-Peak Performance

### Tell People How They're Doing

There is a story of a man in a restaurant making a phone call. "Mr. Smith?" he said, "I understand you have been looking for an assistant." He paused. "Oh, you hired one two months ago and are pleased with your choice. Well, thank you anyway. I hope you continue to be satisfied with your decision."

When he hung up the phone, the restaurant manager commented, "I happened to overhear your conversation. I'm sorry you didn't get a shot at the job."

"Oh, that's all right," the man replied. "That's my boss. I was hired as his assistant three months ago. I was just phoning to find out how I'm doing."

*- The Speaker's Sourcebook*


## Raise Expectations

Experience proves that the higher your expectations for the performance of your people, the greater will be your people, the greater will be your results. Leaders must have faith in their troops.

The young General Douglas MacArthur demonstrated this principle in France during World War I. Before a deadly charge, MacArthur called the battalion commander to him. "Major," he said, "When the sign comes to go over the top, I want you to go first, before your men. If you do, they'll follow."

MacArthur promptly removed his own Distinguished Service Cross and pinned it on the major. He had awarded the major a medal for heroism he hadn't committed yet. "Now I know you're going to do it," said MacArthur.

When the order came to go over the top, the major was psychologically ready. Proudly wearing his new decoration, he charged out ahead of his troops. The men followed bravely, and the attack achieved its objective.

*- The Speaker's Sourcebook*

## Creating New Realities

In college we used to sell coupon books door-to-door, and we used to have a term, "Create our own reality." This meant that as soon as someone broke a sales record, it changed our entire outlook on our job. For *example*: If the record was 20 coupon books in four hours (a typical work day) and someone broke the record and sold 25, we were no longer happy if we sold 20. Why? Because we realized it was now possible to sell more.

Every day we were trying to create a new reality. The same story is true of the Russian Olympian Vasily Alexeev. He was trying to break a weightlifting record of 500 lbs. He had lifted 499 but couldn't, for the life of him, lift 500.

Finally, his trainers put 501.5 lbs. on his bar and rigged it so it looked like 499 lbs. Of course, you know the story. He lifted it easily. Once he created this new reality, other weightlifters went on to break his record. Why? Because they now knew it was possible to lift 500 lbs. The limits we set for ourselves exist in our minds. Sometimes, if we let our hearts do the talking and believe in our ability to overcome past perceptions, we can create another reality.

*- The Speaker's Sourcebook*

## CEOs on Empowerment

In all organizations there are lots of people just waiting for you to give them some responsibility, some sense of ownership, something they can take personal pride in. Once you do, a thousand flowers will bloom.

- General Bill Creech, USAF

The more you encourage people to take initiative, the more you multiply your own effectiveness.

- Robert Haas, Levi Strauss

Develop a positive organizational climate. Once you do, employees will increase their productivity by 10, 20, 30, and even up to 300%.

- James Burke, Johnson & Johnson

Empowering managers create climates for innovation. They see their most important work as enabling their employees to succeed.

- Larry Perlman, Control Data

The way employees treat customers reflects the manner in which they are treated by management.

- James Perkins, Federal Express

# 8

---

# Mentoring

*"Children need models more than they need critics."*

*Voice for Health*

Who has had the greatest influence on your life, other than a parent or spouse? When asked that question, many employees will point to a leader at work as being responsible for their development. One of the fatal mistakes made by managers is their failure to develop people. John Maxwell is credited with saying, "The one who influences others to follow is only a leader with certain limitations. The one who influences others to lead is a leader without limitations."

## THE KEY TO SUCCESSFUL EMPLOYEE DEVELOPMENT

Mentoring teaches the fundamentals and core values of your business and provides a quality learning environment. The key to successful employee development is communicating the vision and values, then seeing that each employee lives the vision and exemplifies the values. Loyalty is welded in place by mentors, who share their company's philosophy with others on a daily basis.

Never underestimate the power of employees. From hourly workers to managers, they want greater challenges and opportunities to contribute to your organization. They want a stake in the Company. Mentoring creates that sense of ownership and attitude, "what I do *does* make a difference."

Employees learn from those who have been with the company longer; who have more experience in the field; or who have a fresh, creative view of things. Learning is a never-ending cycle; it's natural for employees to want to help others — and that's what mentoring is all about. People have to feel that they work in a caring environment that nurtures them and in which they are acknowledged for helping colleagues.

> **F**reedom is not worth having if it does not connote freedom to err.
> - Mahatma Gandhi

## THE MENTORING PROCESS

### Before Mentoring Begins:

1.  Make sure that you have the right assumptions about people:
    - almost everyone wants to feel important
    - almost everyone has something significant to contribute
    - almost everyone is naturally motivated
    - almost everyone needs someone to show them how to succeed
    - almost everyone wants to succeed

2.  Make sure you embody the kind of behavior and thinking you want. People do what people see. Lead by example and clearly explain what expectations you want.

3.  Make sure your employees fit the task. Know your people well.

Without getting to know employees as individuals, managers cannot hope to realize their full potential. The use of behavioral assessments to help managers better understand themselves and others is strongly suggested. Strengths and weaknesses can be objectively determined and utilized or managed more effectively. Sharing of assessments with one management level up, down, and horizontally also has proven value in leadership training.

> **U**nderpromise — Overperform.

## The Art of Mentoring:

1.  Cultivate a personal relationship. You can impress from a distance, but you have to be up close to have impact.

    ■ mentoring occurs best in the context of a one-on-one relationship
    ■ mentoring occurs best in informal settings
    ■ mentoring occurs best when the mentoree feels cared for
    ■ mentoring occurs best when a mentoree can observe his/ her mentor living out the values and principles in everyday situations

2.  Move mentorees through a four-step training strategy.

    ■ I do, you watch (observation and modeling)    *Directing*
    ■ I do, you help (limited participation)    *Coaching*
    ■ You do, I help (assistance and evaluation)    *Supporting*
    ■ You do, I do (encouragement) *Delegating Empowerment*

Training needs to be paced and needs based. Make sure that you also help them develop their people and attitude skills. Then repeat, repeat, repeat.

3.  Provide the resources they need for successful achievement.

4.  Help them visualize who they can become.

    ■ help them see who they are
    ■ help them see how they can fit with the teams' vision

5.  Build their self-esteem.

    ■ people improve better with positive reinforcement
    ■ praise needs to be specific and sincere
    ■ praise needs to be constant
    ■ praise works best when written and/or in public
    ■ listen to mentorees and their ideas. Listening says, "I value"

6.  Create a safe environment, an atmosphere where it's OK to make mistakes.

    ■ failure is the back door to success
    ■ people usually learn more from failure than success

7. Hold them accountable.

- schedule regular meetings for ongoing reporting/encouragement
- confront when needed (in private)
- agree on areas of further development (set goals and standards)
- check back with them informally along the way

8. Take on additional protégés.

Downsizing, early retirements, and reengineering of companies have literally destroyed mentoring. Long-term success in corporations came from a cadre of older employees guiding young employees. Today, the older employees are no longer, in strength and number, employed and mentorship has suffered. Leaders have to step up to the plate and take their place.

## MY PERSONAL MENTORS

Leaders are trained, not born. I've been fortunate to have several mentors, who have had much to do in shaping my leadership style, values and beliefs, and ultimately my attitude and personal behavior. I am grateful for the help I received, and I have reciprocated by helping other young, aspiring leaders along the way. Here's who helped me and how they helped me:

> Children are 25% of our population and 100% of our future.

Harry Beatty was a 33-year-old mid-level administrator at Fairchild Industries when I first met him in 1963. Harry dropped out of high school and shortly thereafter, he married and started a family. He began his career as a draftsman. His career languished until Fairchild tested hundreds of engineers, including Harry, and learned of his high IQ. He was given increased responsibility and quickly advanced to the position he had when I met him.

Harry encouraged me to get my Masters' Degree in engineering administration prior to raising a family. Because of his persistence,

I enrolled at The George Washington University in September, 1964 and received my MEA in June, 1967. My first child, Lisa, was born on June 29, 1967.

Dr. Coleman Raphael was General Manager of Fairchild's Space and Electronics Division. I directly reported to him. Coleman, who received his doctorate shortly after arriving at Fairchild, had a photographic memory and would regularly leave his office to meet with employees at their workstations or desks. He knew each employee by name and would always ask them about work improvements and more importantly, their families. Morale was very high and people gave 100% while he was at Fairchild.

Coleman was caring and sensitive and showed a personal interest in my career. He named me as Fairchild's representative to the Montgomery County, Maryland Chamber of Commerce. By age 31, I became President of the Chamber. Shortly afterwards, I became involved with Holy Cross Hospital, and over many years I served the hospital as a volunteer including Board of Trustees Chairman, and President and Chairman of the hospital's Mens' Guild — their fund-raising arm. More recently, I also served as Chairman of the Advisory Board for The Academy of the Holy Cross, a Catholic girls' highschool sponsored by The Sisters of Holy Cross.

My active community involvement is a result of Coleman Raphael's encouragement and interest in me. He also exemplified a professional work ethic that I have followed in my own career — the importance of being punctual and having a good attendance record. I've never been late to work, or for a meeting, and missed only 4 days of work in 34 years. I'm proud of that achievement.

Ed Friedman, PE, was a partner with Connell, Pierce, Gartlan and Friedman, when I met him in 1967. He was nearing retirement age at the time. His firm performed architectural/engineering services for Fairchild and I was the Owner's Representative.

On one of my initial visits, I was admiring his many awards in his office and he told me that if I were interested, he would spend time with me after work and mentor me. Of course, I accepted his offer and he spent many hours with me talking about what he did to receive recognition. Mr. Friedman, now deceased, was named Consulting Engineer of the Year on two separate occasions in his career, and today, The American Society of Civil Engineers' top award is named in his honor.

Ed Friedman encouraged me to write technical articles for publication and to speak at national conferences. Within a year, I had seven articles published and one speaking engagement, which terrified me. To date, I've published over 60 articles; including six cover features; was a contributing author of a book, *High Tech Real Estate*; and have authored two books. I've spoken extensively on such subjects as management, leadership, leasing, telecommunications, facilities management, getting recognition, motivation, and attitude. I've also been fortunate to have been selected for 30 national awards.

John Toups, PE was Chairman and President/CEO of Planning Research Corporation in McLean, VA and was my boss for 6 ½ years, from 1978 to 1985. I was Corporate Director of Facilities and Administrative Services at the time, reporting directly to him. He interviewed and hired me prior to joining PRC. I vividly recall being asked to take two days of psychological testing, including an IQ test, with Dr. Art Annis, then department head of psychology at UCLA. I appreciate and value that experience. Chemistry and "people skills" were important to PRC and all executives were tested prior to being offered executive-level positions.

John Toups taught me the importance of having everyone participate and how to encourage employee involvement. He gave me the freedom and opportunity to fail, which not many executives do. He also taught me how to delegate and empower employees.

William Hussmann was Chief Administrative Officer for Montgomery County, MD where I spent two separate, short careers as Director of Facilities and Services (between 1972 and 1978 and 1991 and 1994). Bill taught me the value of TRUST. He also gave me the authority and freedom to get the job done and cheered me on to whatever successes resulted from my efforts. During my last three-year stint, I was allowed to put my leadership principles to work in government, the results of which are contained in my book, *Looking for The Gold — A TQM Success Story.*

Zig Ziglar is highly reputed to be the world's best teacher of motivation. I first heard Zig in 1991 and I currently facilitate two of his training programs — "See You At The Top" and "Strategies For Success." I have found these training programs to be invaluable as fundamental training for all employees and have taught or exposed at least 6000 people to his programs. Zig Ziglar encouraged me to write my first book. I value his friendship and mentorship deeply.

---

### Lesson in Leadership

Jean-Claude Killy said: "The best and fastest way to learn a sport is to watch and imitate a champion." Associate with positive people and learn leadership from the experience of those who have reached the top.

Great companies such as Procter & Gamble assign mentors to all new professional employees. Don't wait to be assigned a mentor. Ask someone in your organization, who you respect, to be your mentor. Mentoring will get you to the top quicker than any other management tool available.

# SUCCESS STORIES

### Paying Back Uncle Joe

When newscaster Bernard Meltzer was putting himself through college he was accepted by tuition-free CCNY in New York City but lacked $100 to pay for books. He took his problem to a friend of the family he called Uncle Joe.

Uncle Joe listened to the problem and wrote a check for $100. Meltzer was overwhelmed and said, "I don't know when I can pay you back the money..."

Uncle Joe replied. "You can never give me back the money, Bernard. I will not accept it. However, there will come a time in the future when you will be successful. And someone will come to you for help. You must leave your door open and you must listen, and you must try to be of assistance. And then you can say, 'I'm paying back Uncle Joe...'"

- *Up the Loyalty Ladder*, Murray Raphel
and Neil Raphel, Harper Business, New York, NY

### Hang in There...

- The greatest quarterbacks complete only 6 out of 10 passes.
- The best basketball players make only about 50% of their shots.
- Major-league baseball players make it to first base only 25% of the time — and that includes walks.
- Top oil companies, even with the help of expert geologists, must dig an average of 10 wells before finding oil.
- A successful actor is turned down 29 out of 30 times after auditioning for roles in TV commercials.
- Winners in the stock market make money on only 2 out of every 5 investments.

- *The Joy of Working*, by Dennis Waitley

## The Wisdom of the Ages

The old-timers have a lot of wisdom to share. If the universal mentor could talk, he or she might say...

*"The strongest human emotion is neither love nor hate but the unquenchable urge to share a secret."* Never talk about confidential matters in the elevator, rest rooms, or anywhere you can be overheard. The person who overhears could be a competitor, a client, or the new vice president.

*"Share the credit."* It makes your coworkers feel good and it makes you look good. *"If you don't know the answer to a question, say 'I don't know.'"* If you make a mistake, admit it. If you owe someone an apology, apologize. Don't guess, don't bluff, don't bluster.

*"If you get in over your head, never be too scared to admit it."* The rule of thumb is, if you think you're in trouble, you probably are. So don't let the situation snowball. Ask for help.

*"Don't discuss salaries with your peers."* If they find out you're making more than they are, there will be jealousy and bitterness. The only people who need to know your salary are you, your supervisor, and the personnel department.

*"Don't underestimate your boss's knowledge, intelligence, or awareness of what's going on."* Never confuse tact with ignorance.

*"Be nice to people you don't particularly like, especially if you outrank them."* Very few truly nasty people get ahead.

*"Don't be afraid to get your hands dirty."* Better to clear the coffee cups after a meeting than to sit there and watch the CEO start doing it.

*"Take your lumps."* Life isn't always fair. Somebody else may get the promotion you deserve, the office you covet, more credit than you for a job well done. Don't whine about it. Accept the knocks with grace. It won't go unnoticed.

*"Try very hard not to say, 'I told you so'"* ever.

- Michael Maxtone-Graham, writing in *Training*, Lakewood Publications, Inc.

## Lead by Example

Managing people is difficult and time-consuming work, done best by kindness, watching, warning, patience, praise, and — above all — by example.

Any person in a management or supervisory position is basically a salesperson. It's your job to sell good attitudes and good work habits. If you don't practice them yourself, it's a hard sale to make — sometimes impossible. People judge you more by what you do than by what you say.

Good executives appreciate that the power of a good example is one of their most effective tools. They know that people are watching them as they go about their daily work, and that their own example will influence those people far more than verbal advice or preaching.

Some people feel that when they have reached an executive level they are no longer subject to the same standards they expect of others. They think it's their job to tell people what to do, regardless of whether they do it themselves or not. But if they don't believe in something enough to practice it themselves, the telling seldom does much good.

The strengths and weaknesses of a particular department often reflect the strengths and weaknesses of the man or woman who runs it. When you have difficulty getting people who work for you to measure up to the standards you insist upon, take a second look at yourself. Do you measure up to these standards? Are you practicing them whole-heartedly in your own work, or just preaching for the benefit of others?

If you habitually let down and take it easy when your own manager is away, how can you expect your own people to act any differently when you're not around?

If you're usually late yourself, how can you expect others to be on time? The words will go in one ear and out the other.

What's sauce for the goose is sauce for the gander. If you want to be an effective leader, you'd better believe that — it's the way people are made. If you want them to buy something, be sure you're buying it yourself first.

Never underestimate the importance of a good example. Seeing is believing.

*- The Working Communicator*

# 9

## Communicating

*"It is the province of knowledge to speak and it is the privilege of wisdom to listen."*

Oliver Wendell Holmes, Jr.

Beginning in November 1958, Thomas J. Watson, Jr. shared the IBM vision by communicating regularly with all levels of management through a publication called *Management Briefing*. The basic purpose of the publication was to provide managers throughout the company with more background information about current IBM announcements and activities and explain, to the greatest possible degree, the "why" behind the policies. In addition, it contained, from time to time actual case studies which had an object lesson for the benefit of all management. He was always concerned about getting too large and too bureaucratic and communication became one of IBM's largest hurdles to overcome. No one is better than IBM in communicating with their managers, and through their managers, to all their people.

### EMPLOYEES NUMBER ONE COMPLAINT

In my book, *Looking for the Gold*, I devoted a chapter to communicating and used IBM's methodology, which was to include memos and other important messages and expectations that I wrote to my management team and associates. *Employees' number one complaint is that their managers do not communicate well or enough with them.*

115

Other common employee complaints are that they are not well informed about what's happening in the company and they do not feel they are as involved as they should be in the company.

## FACE-TO-FACE COMMUNICATIONS

Managers should spend over 50% of their time communicating the information needed to conduct their business and to motivate their people. Studies have indicated that "face-to-face" communication, with opportunities for discussion and questions, is generally preferred.

There are many components to a strong communications system including one-on-one encounters and discussions, meetings, memos, written policies, procedures and manuals, training, recognition — both positive and negative — and example. More recently, we could add technological developments such as voice mail and e-mail.

> The best way to get top performance from your people is to let them know how they are doing before they have to ask.

Communications training in each component is necessary, since it takes more than words to communicate. It *takes* commitment to one's words by one's action.

## EFFECTIVE WAYS TO TRAIN AND IMPROVE YOUR COMMUNICATIONS SKILLS

Communicating is not just a manager's job — it is everyone's responsibility. The manager cannot solve everyone's problems.

> One machine can do the work of fifty ordinary men. No machine can do the work of one extraordinary man.
> - Elbert Hubbard

One of the most effective ways to improve communications is to hold meetings often with all your employees. There is *no* substitute for regular sessions in which ideas can be exchanged.

Initially, your meetings will not produce much give and take, but don't get discouraged. When employees become convinced that your meetings will be regular and that you sincerely want people to speak up and will give their ideas serious attention, they will speak out. The right communications' environment is the "on-the-job" atmosphere that says, *"management is listening."*

Managers would also do well to encourage employees to "educate their boss" and communicate up the organization. Management's obligation is to learn what their people want and fear, and to help people get what they want and to help them overcome their

> **W**hen your work speaks for itself, don't interrupt.
> - Henry J. Kaiser

fears. One of our greatest fears is public speaking, but with encouragement from management, employees can learn to speak publicly. Once they do, their road to success will be much easier, since they will develop or reinforce their confidence and self-esteem.

Let me share the following example with you. A few years ago, I identified fifteen people in my department as "rising stars" and strongly felt that a course in public speaking, such as those offered by Dale Carnegie or Toastmasters' International, would be very helpful in their personal development. I recognized that because of their fear of public speaking, they would unlikely volunteer for this type of training. So I sent them each a personal letter indicating how proud I was to be working with them, talked about their potential and how important I thought public speaking would be to their future development, and ended by telling them that I was nominating them to take a full year's Toastmasters' Program at the company's expense. It wouldn't cost them a dime. Our department would pick up the dues and associated costs.

Under these circumstances, each of them enrolled (even though I knew that they immensely disliked what I had done) and not only finished the program, but also re-enrolled at their expense for the second year. What started in their minds as a punishment became a promotable skill which they all are happy to have. Five

> **T**he word communication comes from the Latin *communico*, meaning share.

of six officers of the Montgomery County Toastmasters' Club, including the president in 1995/1996, were my associates.

Leaders must be able to communicate effectively. Communication is the sharing of meaning. True communication is analogous to an electrical circuit — the information we are trying to share is the electricity, our presentation of it is the wire and the light bulb has to come on for communication to take place. If the light bulb does not come on, communication is not happening.

Communicating like a leader is not the same as giving effective presentations. Although proper communication techniques are helpful, principle is more important. Credibility is the root of leadership. Leaders tell it like it is, and speak with passion and energy from the heart. They are authentic, honest and model daily the behaviors and actions that are visibly congruent with their spoken words. Consistent actions communicate with amazing clarity.

> Society is on the side of the giver.
> - Zig Ziglar

## IT'S HOW YOU SAY IT THAT MATTERS

Since what you have to say makes up less than forty percent of communicating, oral communication is the best way to communicate. *It's how you say what you say that is important.* There is a direct correlation between individual success and the ability to communicate (and commanding a large vocabulary).

One of my most difficult problems was how to say "no" to others. I didn't want to hurt employees' or customers' feelings or make them feel unimportant. In certain instances, I could not always accommodate their requests and said "no," but with an explanation, generally done face-to-face. People would ask me to take on more responsibility even though they knew I was over-committed, because they also knew, if they persisted that I would eventually say "yes." I've overcome this problem, but it isn't easy and I still wrestle with it, because I love hearing the compliment, "Give the job to Migs, he'll get it done."

> Remember that a person's name to that person is the sweetest and most important sound in any language.
> - Dale Carnegie

All good performance starts with clear goals. Without clear goals you will quickly become a victim, because you will have no framework to make decisions about where you should or shouldn't focus your energy. I've become much better at saying "no" when I am clearer about my focus and goals.

> The tongue is the only thing that gets sharper with use.
>
> - Washington Irving

The following are two approaches I've used to say "no":

**Be clear and realistic about the consequences of doing one more thing.** This advice is for both yourself and for the person who wants you to do something new. I've learned that the best approach is to be honest and direct. For example, say, "If I do this, I won't be able to get to the other things that I've committed to." If for no other reason than past history, you can say, "With what I've got going on right now, I feel certain that I won't do as good a job as I'd like and we will both be disappointed."

In recent years, when a new opportunity comes my way I often compliment the idea (if I feel it has merit) and then simply say, "I don't choose to get involved." I've found this to be a powerful approach. Most people don't question it, they accept it and say "Thank you."

**Offer alternatives and solutions.** Suggest someone else who you feel could do a better job or who is available sooner to work on the task. If the request comes from your manager, suggest that a project or priority that you are doing that could be dropped, delayed or given to someone else, or ask him or her to do the same.

The degree of flexibility between these approaches is a function of exactly what the task is, who's asking that you take it on, and the time frame involved. A request from your senior management is going to involve more consideration and discussion than a request from an associate or someone you don't know.

> It is the province of knowledge to speak and it is the privilege of wisdom to listen.
>
> - Oliver Wendell Holmes

# COLLABORATIVE COMMUNICATION

We always communicate. What we fail to do is to communicate effectively. There is no doubt that effective communication skills are important and tomorrow's workplace will require even better communication skills. In this age of empowerment and downsizing (especially at the middle management level), sharing of information with employees is essential. How can people be involved and contribute to something they know little about?

I spoke earlier of the importance of public speaking, and of equal importance is written communication. Every organization conducts substantial business in writing, exchanging information through proposals, letters, memos, instructions, reports, and more recently, e-mail. Many college graduates, including MBAs from respected institutions, have never taken a business writing course, and lack necessary skills to put their thoughts concisely on paper. Seminars in business communication can help close the written communication skill gap we have in America today.

As I see it, the biggest impediment to effective communication skills is ensuring that your message is heard and understood, which requires collaborative communication skills. Most people are so wrapped up in the content of what they are attempting to communicate that they don't recognize if their message is being received and understood. If your receiver hasn't understood the message, agreed with it and interpreted it according to your intent, you have no communication. We should learn how to recognize what our communication partner needs to receive information.

Listening skills are an important ingredient of the solution to ensure that what we say is heard. Your ability to listen will communicate how much you care far more clearly than any words you may say. And when it's your turn to speak, the other person will listen with equal intensity. Asking questions is an often overlooked or underutilized part of the listening process. It will expand your knowledge and deepen your insights and level of understanding. Teaching listening skills will produce significant bottom line results.

People don't communicate poorly on purpose. For the most part they are unaware of their problems unless they get feedback.

If you aren't getting it, ask for feedback. The purpose of feedback is to gather perceptions from other people about your behavior. What others perceive has a profound impact on their relationship with you, on how well they will cooperate with you, and how willing they will respond to you as a leader.

Today's hot topic is electronic communication. Countless hours are being spent on teaching workers how to communicate with modems, intranets, and the Internet. What we seem to forget is that there is no substitute for human interface. Employees would much prefer hearing directly from their supervisors and coworkers than an electronic bulletin board or e-mail. Electronic communication has its place, as does the written word. It gives one the options of addressing many people at the same time and is generally the quickest and most expedient thing to do. However the ability to inform and persuade a listener face to face, one-on-one, remains the most effective and important communication skill.

---

### Lesson in Leadership

Look carefully at your organization and notice where the executive offices are located. Are they easily accessible to where you sit? Do leaders in your company regularly mix in with employees? Have you met the executives of your company? Do they know you by name?

If the answers to the above questions are all "yes," that's terrific! Regrettably, that won't be the answer for over 90% of you. Employees' greatest complaint is that their managers do not communicate or communicate often enough with them.

Your job as a leader is to communicate a lot (over 50% of your time) and do it on a face to face basis because "it's not what you say, but how you say it" that counts.

## *SUCCESS STORIES*

### Your Face Says It All

The great theologian, Charles H. Spurgeon, was teaching his class the finer points of public speaking. He emphasized the importance of making the facial expression harmonize with the speech.

"When you speak of heaven," he said, "let your face light up, let it be irradiated with a heavenly gleam, let your eyes shine with reflected glory. But when you speak of hell — well, then your ordinary face will do."

It is amazing how vividly we wear our attitude on our face, and we are responsible for the message it delivers.

During the days of Lincoln's presidency, a trusted adviser recommended a candidate for the Lincoln cabinet. Lincoln briefly considered the possibility before declining to make the appointment. When asked why, he said, "I don't like the man's face."

"But the poor man is not responsible for his face," Lincoln's adviser pleaded.

"Every man over forty is responsible for his face," Lincoln insisted, and the prospect was considered no further.

*The outward expression on our face bears the hidden truths of our heart.*

*- The Speaker's Sourcebook*

# 10

---

# Developing Your
# Leadership Potential

*"Do unto others as they would like done unto them."*

*The Platinum Rule*, Tony Alessandra

Today's managers are vastly different than those who reigned 10 years ago. Leaders now need a host of new people skills in order to effectively deal with fast-paced technological changes, the aftermath of corporate downsizing and constant productivity increase demands by top management.

Since 1990, my profession, facilities management — and especially maintenance — has taken the brunt of early retirements and downsizing (made in the good name of TQM/CQI), and we lost many leaders and role models in the process. Compounding the problem, top management froze hiring, deferred maintenance even further, and has demanded continuous productivity increases from the remaining staff.

In many cases, top management listened to the advice of outsiders and outsourced or co-sourced the facilities management function and fortunately for us, most of these decisions were made in haste and without much study. Hence, it is possible to reverse the trend we've experienced thus far in the 1990s.

## FIFTEEN WAYS TO DEVELOP/REINFORCE YOUR LEADERSHIP SKILLS

### 1. Accept the Challenge

As we approach the beginning of the next millennium we should recognize that there will be fewer well-paying jobs available and older managers with obsolete skills will have to better prepare themselves in order to compete successfully. Much of the downsizing that has occurred in the 1990s has affected middle management the most, and companies are looking for leaders to emerge to replace that eliminated layer of management — leaders who can instill in their employees the attitudes and feelings that they can and will accomplish objectives that enhance productivity as well as their personal and professional lives.

Productivity is the name of the game. Those who master productivity will not only survive, but also thrive, and even in the most trying circumstances, there are several things you can do right now that will give you a jump start and bring out the leader within you.

### 2. Think Big and Positive

Over the past five years we've been conditioned to believe that we are helpless and can't do anything about it. The greatest challenge you have is to be the best you can be and unleash your and your employees' fullest potential. Your success has to do with thinking big and thinking positively.

Have a vision and share it with others. Henry Ford once said, *"If you think you can or you can't, you're right."* If you can impart the "I can" philosophy in those around you, you'll be on the right track. *Nothing constructive can be done unless you think positively.*

### 3. Know the Business of Your Business

Understand how your job and your department fits into the company as a whole. Learn how your boss sees your job and don't be afraid to ask him or her that question. Then concentrate your efforts on those things deemed most important by the boss and/or by the customer. The following employer "needs" may be of help to you in asking the right questions and help point you in the right direction:

- People who adapt fast
- People who "buy in" and embrace change
- People who have a sense of urgency
- People who accept ambiguity and uncertainty
- People who behave as if it were their business
- People who keep on learning
- People who hold themselves accountable
- People who add value — who contribute much more than they cost
- People who get close to their customer
- People who manage their own morale, i.e., self-motivated
- People who continuously improve
- People who are solution-oriented, not finger-pointers
- People who change before they have to

Senior executives at DuPont, for example, talk about the company's future and say they want their leaders to develop people to their fullest potential, develop positive attitudes, and create voluntary changes in people's behavior. They also talk about the importance of a balanced work life, sharing information (training), accepting the magnitude of change, and interdependency. And they advise their people to stop living in the past. DuPont is now focusing on success-based employment and no longer on security as a guiding principle.

### 4. Become Indispensable by Educating Your Boss

Many of us assume that our boss knows and appreciates what we do. That's not the case. Send regular reports to your boss on the many value-based contributions of your department, such as highlighting savings achieved, increasing life span of equipment, reducing energy, increasing indoor air quality, etc. Concentrate on value and bottom-line contributions. Often it is helpful to videotape before and after conditions of maintenance and other projects to illustrate accomplishments and quality. We've got to get better at selling ourselves and our accomplishments.

### 5. Invest in Yourself and Others

Invest in training for you and your people. Most people use the excuse that training dollars were dropped from the budget.

Investment in training will pay for itself several times over within the first year, so there is little to no risk involved. What you spend in training will reduce your overall budget every time. Why, then, do we continue to skimp on training?

### 6. Focus Training on the Human Element

It is people who are the essential ingredient in coordinating time and products, use the time and manage the resources. By focusing training on the human element and on "mindset" issues, significant results can be obtained and training that impacts behavior will enable real change. I have found that Zig Ziglar's "Strategies For Success" training system is the best training resource to use for this purpose.

### 7. Increase Your Visibility

Volunteer for projects in your company that nobody wants and do a great job on them. Some examples are U.S. Savings Bond Drive, United Way, and other charity drives. Also, volunteer in the community and become a community leader. Lastly, champion projects important to the company and your boss. Always be visible in support of your boss.

### 8. Involve Your Employees

Confucius taught an important lesson many years ago and we need to learn the lesson. *"If you tell people something, they'll forget; if you show them, they'll remember; if you involve them, they'll understand."* Don't ever underestimate the power of employees.

### 9. Increase Your Ability to Deal with Change

A leader must be able to cope with adversity as his or her company undergoes change. Don't be overwhelmed by our increasingly changing world. You not only have to adapt to change, but also have to become an agent for change.

### 10. Bring Back Values

It is vital for a leader to have honesty, credibility, ethical behavior, integrity, candor, and sensitivity — a leader who cares. Cavett Robert says, *"People don't care how much you know until they know how much you care."* Positive, caring environments are characteristic of all successful companies. Many studies have shown that productivity is always much higher in companies that develop and nurture these environments. People who feel good about themselves always produce more and with better quality. People with values, in combination with a positive but aggressive attitude, will never tolerate being in second place in any marketplace.

## 11. Financial Know-How

Today's manager must understand financial statements and the impact of their operation on the bottom line. They must also be proficient in presenting their value to the organization financially. A dollar saved in operations today equates to about $20 in sales. Being able to communicate well, incorporating numbers that affect the bottom line, will make a positive difference in how you are perceived by top management.

## 12. Value Diversity

Diversity is the differences that make each individual unique. Learn to address situations in a multicultural environment that will guard against prejudice and maintain good relationships.

## 13. Be Decisive and Be Bold

Good judgment anchored by prudent risk taking are qualities found in leaders who act boldly with courage, tenacity and persistence. Leaders don't procrastinate and aren't afraid to make decisions (many of us won't give ourselves permission to be wrong).

## 14. Develop a Sense of Urgency

A fine art of management is the ability to communicate a sense of urgency to employees who work with you without haranguing or being unpleasant about it. Let your employees know how important having a sense of urgency is to you, to them and to the customer.

## 15. Look for the Gold in Others

People want to be recognized. Why don't we heed this advice? Do these things and become a finder of the good in others. It's the most important lesson that we can learn. *When we become "other-people" centered, we will receive the true rewards of life.* That's what leadership is all about. More than anything, it will help bring out the full potential of the employee.

Downsizing of the 1990s has decimated the trust and loyalty of employees — qualities, which are so essential to maximizing productivity. The responsibility is yours — you are the coach. Do everything possible as a role model manager. Make your employees' jobs easier and make them feel good, remembering that people who feel good about themselves produce good results. The key to top performance is feeling good, feeling valuable. If employees feel good, they'll be excited about their work and about accomplishing things without being supervised or prodded.

Try to catch someone doing good and recognize that good in a timely manner. This harnesses the proven concept of the Pygmalion effect, a powerful factor in behavioral change, i.e., *whenever the leader truly believes a group can fulfill his/her expectations, it happens.* People do rise to the level of others around them. Surround yourself with positive, successful people.

It is recommended that you keep these steps of developing leadership within easy reading distance. Review and use them often. They will help you positively change the organizational culture of your department. Developing and maintaining a positive, caring work environment is the only way to motivate and build better people. They, in turn, will produce a return on the investment that you placed in them a hundredfold. Remember, what goes around comes around.

---

### Lesson in Leadership

Your potential is almost unlimited. You already have in you some of every quality of success needed to be whatever you want to be, to do whatever you want to do, and to have whatever you want to have. All you need to do now is to make the decision to refine/reinforce your qualities to move closer toward your goal of becoming a successful leader.

You can sit back, complain about how unfair life is, make excuses and watch the world pass you by. Or you can stand up, step forward, boldly take on each challenge that comes your way, and do whatever it takes to become the best you can be. It's your choice.

## What's In, What's Out

| IN | OUT |
|---|---|
| Post-Heroic Leadership | Heroic Leadership |
| (a.k.a.) | (a.k.a.) |
| Shared Leadership | Coveted Leadership |
| Distributive Leadership | Possessive Leadership |
| Syndicated Leadership | Monopoly Leadership |
| Servant Leadership | "Lorded" Leadership |
| Virtual Leadership | Absolute Leadership |
| Transformative Leadership | Stagnant Leadership |
| Leadership by Inspiration | Leadership by Perspiration |
| Conceptual Controls | Procedural Controls |
| Leaders | Managers |
| Coaches | Bosses/Chiefs/Supervisors |
| Unmanaged | Managed |
| Theory Y | Theory X |
| Associates | Employees |
| Partners | Contractors |
| Teams | Divisions |
| Workouts | Meetings |
| Affinity Groups | Cliques |
| Participation | Isolation |
| Empowerment | Mandates |
| Boundaryless | Hierarchies |
| Vision Statements | Mission Statements |
| Shared Values | Rules/Regulations |

Compiled/created by Jay Kenney, PhD

# SUCCESS STORIES

## The Lincoln Legacy

When failure continually knocks at your door, welcome it in. Once experienced and learned from, failure becomes the stepping stone to success.

Consider a man whose life was engulfed with failure, setbacks, and letdowns. He once wrote, "I am the most miserable man living. Whether I shall be better, I cannot tell."

He experienced a difficult childhood. When he was only seven years old, his family was forced out of their home on a legal technicality. He went to work to support his family, and at nine, his mother died. He completed less than one year of formal schooling.

At twenty-two, he lost his job as a store clerk. His desire was to go to law school, but his lack of education restricted him from being admitted. He borrowed money to become a partner in a small business. A few years later, his partner died, leaving him swamped in debt that took him seventeen years to repay.

In 1832, he was defeated for the legislature; this was followed by another business failure one year later.

In 1835, the young woman he loved refused to marry him, and a woman he had loved earlier died, leaving him rejected, confused, and heartbroken.

He was defeated for speaker in 1838 and defeated for the elector in 1840. Two years later he married into a burdensome life and an ultimately unhappy relationship.

He was defeated for Congress in 1843, but finally, after his third try, was elected in 1846. Two years later, at thirty-nine, he ran again and failed to be reelected.

His personal life was also in shambles. His four-year-old son died. (In fact, only one of his four sons lived past eighteen.) At this point, he experienced a nervous breakdown. The next year, he failed to get an appointment to the U.S. Land Office.

At forty-five, he ran and was badly defeated for the U.S. Senate. Two years later, in 1856, he became a candidate for the vice presidency and again experienced defeat.

Failure stood at his door in 1858 when he was again badly defeated for the U.S. Senate.

Amazingly enough, this man withstood a lifetime of crisis, criticism, public denial, personal defeat, deep depression, and loneliness to become a U.S. President in 1860. At fifty-one years old, he experienced the success he so badly desired. However, his second term of office was cut short by a final earthly defeat — his assassination.

As Abraham Lincoln lay dying, Edwin M. Stanton spoke of this man as most of us remember him: "There lies the most perfect ruler of men the world has ever seen ... [and] now he belongs to the ages."

Because of his accomplishments, his foresight, his insight, and his wisdom, Abraham Lincoln was an example of how failure can produce achievement.

Lincoln would surely have agreed with Charles F. Kettering, who believed, "It is not a disgrace to fail. Failing is one of the greatest arts in the world."

*- The Speaker's Sourcebook*

## Flying Further

Observe closely the beautiful Canadian geese flying in their V-formation. Have you ever wondered why one wing of the V is longer than the other wing of the V? (Answer: The longer wing has more geese.)

Seriously, the geese instinctively know the value of cooperation. Did you know that they regularly change leadership? Why? The leader fights the head wind, helping to create a partial vacuum for the geese on his right, as well as the geese on the left. When he becomes exhausted, another goose takes over.

Scientists have discovered in wind tunnel tests that a flock of geese can fly 72 percent farther and faster by cooperating in this manner. People can do the same thing. People must cooperate with, instead of fighting against, their fellow men.

*- Zig Ziglar*

## Small Efforts Make A Big Difference

As the old man walked down a Spanish beach at dawn, he saw ahead of him what he thought to be a dancer. A young man was running across the sand rhythmically, bending down to pick up a stranded starfish and throw it far into the sea. The old man gazed in wonder as the young man again and again threw the small starfish from the sand to the water. The old man approached him and asked why he spent so much energy doing what seemed a waste of time. The young man explained that the stranded starfish would die if left until the morning sun.

"But there must be thousands of miles of beach and millions of starfish. How can your efforts make any difference?"

The young man looked down at the small starfish in his hand and as he threw it to safety in the sea, said, "It makes a difference to this one."

*- The Speaker's Sourcebook*

## Real Success Is Long Term

Since this is the first week of a new baseball season, I thought it would be fitting to open with a story about a homerun-hitting farm boy from my home state of Mississippi. This fellow could hit a baseball a country mile, as they say. So one of the major league teams invited him to spring training.

Each week the young slugger wired his mother. The first week he said, "Dear Mom, leading all batters. These pitchers are not so tough."

A week later he boasted, "Looks like I will be a starting infielder. Now hitting 500."

But early in the third week, the young man's mother got this wire: "Dear Mom," it said, "They started throwing curves. Will be home Friday."

I tell this story to illustrate that success, whether it's baseball or business, is not a one- or two-week hot streak. Real success is long term.

- Earnie Deavenport, President,
Eastman Chemical Company

## Success Is Failure

R.H. Macy failed seven times before his store in New York caught on.

Novelist John Creasey got 753 rejection slips before he published the first of his 564 books.

Thomas Edison was thrown out of school in the early grades when the teachers decided he could not do the work.

Harry S. Truman failed as a haberdasher.

When Bob Dylan performed at a high school talent show, his classmates booed him off the stage.

W. Clement Stone, successful insurance company executive and founder of *Success* magazine, was a high-school dropout.

- *Success* Magazine

## Golden Rule

More than 30 years ago, Ted Williams was closing out his career with the Boston Red Sox. He was suffering from a pinched nerve in his neck that season. "The thing was so bad," he later explained, "that I could hardly turn my head to look at the pitcher."

For the first time in his career he batted under .300, hitting just .254 with 10 home runs. He was the highest salaried player in sports, making $125,000. The next year, the Red Sox sent him the same contract.

When he got the contract, Williams sent it back with a note saying that he would not sign it until they gave him the full pay cut allowed. "I was always treated fairly by the Red Sox when it came to contracts," Williams said. "Now they were offering me a contract I didn't deserve. And I only wanted what I deserved."

Williams cut his own salary by 25%, raised his batting average by 62 points, and closed out a brilliant career by hitting a home run in his final time at bat.

- From a speech by A. Thomas Young,
President and CEO of Martin Marietta Corporation

## What Do People Want?

- Health
- To be important
- To be appreciated
- To be involved
- To have a challenging job
- To have job security

## What Do People Fear?

- Failure
- Rejection
- Confrontation
- Public speaking
- Change

## Age Is No Barrier

- George Burns won his first Oscar at eighty.
- Mickey Mantle hit twenty-three home runs his first full year in the major leagues. He was twenty years old.
- Golda Meir was seventy-one when she became prime minister of Israel.

- William Pitt was only twenty-four when Great Britain called on him to become prime minister.
- George Bernard Shaw was ninety-four when one of his plays was first produced. At ninety-six, he broke his leg when he fell out of a tree he was trimming in his backyard.
- Mozart published his first composition as a seven-year old.
- Grandma Moses didn't start painting until she was eighty years old. She completed over fifteen hundred paintings in the remainder of her life, with 25% of those produced after she was one hundred.
- Benjamin Franklin published his first newspaper column when he was sixteen and had the honor of framing the U.S. Constitution when he was eighty-one.
- Michelangelo was seventy-one when he painted the Cistine Chapel.
- Albert Schweitzer was still performing operations in his African hospital at eighty-nine.
- John D. Rockefeller was making $1 million a week when he died at ninety-three.
- Neither Henry Ford nor Abraham Lincoln realized any success until after they were forty years old.
- Doc Councilman, at fifty-eight, became the oldest person ever to swim the English Channel.
- Gordie Howe remained a top competitor in the National Hockey League into his early fifties.
- S.I. Hayakawa retired as president of San Francisco State University at seventy, and was then elected to the U.S. Senate.
- Herbert Hoover, at eighty-four, served as U.S. Representative to Belgium.
- Winston Churchill assumed the role of Great Britain's prime minister at sixty-five. At seventy, he addressed the crowds on V-E Day, standing on top of his car to speak.
- Charlie Chaplin, at seventy-six, was still directing movies.

- Casey Stengel didn't retire from the rigorous schedule of managing the New York Mets until he was seventy-five.
- Colonel Sanders was sixty-six when Kentucky Fried Chicken became popular.

**There is no need to dread the future or the present. At whatever age, we can be creative, productive, and able to make the most of every day.**

*- The Speaker's Sourcebook*

### Roadmap to Empowerment

To help your team members travel the journey to empowerment, commit yourself to...

- Giving your credit away
- Creating desire instead of fear
- Listening more and talking less
- Keeping your eye on the long term
- Treating every employee like a volunteer
- Speaking from the heart, not just the head
- Telling team members more than they want to know
- Focusing more on customer service and less on the "bottom line"
- Investing in team members so they can become the best they can be
- Sharing your mission, vision, and core values at least six times every day
- Building on people's strengths and accepting their weaknesses
- Trusting customers and team members
- Pushing decision-making down to the lowest level
- Managing by appreciation instead of by exception
- Catching others doing things right
- Leading more and managing less
- Asking more and assigning less

- Making work fun.
- **Remember:** 85% of your success comes from your team members!

> \- Wolf J. Rinke

## Who Said "I Can't"

- Fred Astaire was told after his first screen test that he couldn't act, was slightly bald, and could dance a little.
- Vince Lombardi was told he possessed minimal football knowledge and lacked motivation.
- Louisa May Alcott was advised by her family to find work as a servant or seamstress.
- Beethoven's teacher called him hopeless as a composer.
- Only Enrico Caruso's mother told him he could sing.
- Walt Disney was fired by a newspaper for lacking creativity and went bankrupt several times before Disneyland.
- Publishers turned down Richard Bach's *Jonathan Livingston Seagull*. It sold more than seven million copies in the U.S. alone.
- A Munich schoolmaster told ten-year-old Albert Einstein, "You'll never amount to much."
- Decca Records turned down the Beatles.

> \- *The Motivational Manager*

## Add Value

Make sure you contribute more than you cost.

Employees often mislead themselves, assuming they should get to keep their jobs if they're responsible and do good work. Some of them even have the idea that sticking around for a long time makes them worth more to the organization.

Sure, experience may count for something. But maybe not. It depends on whether that experience really makes you worth more to your employer today, or whether it has mainly lost all value because the world is changing so rapidly.

The "loyalty" issue is a little stickier. People who have shown true devotion over the years — those who have hung in there during tough times and truly worked from the heart, should get points for that. No question, that's a real virtue. That's valuable stuff.

We must realize, however, that we can use history to justify our continued employment for only so long. We still need to add value *now*. And we should not confuse *longevity* with *loyalty*. The mere fact that a person has been on the payroll for years says nothing. You don't get points for just "putting in your time."

It's your *contribution* that counts. Not the hours (or years) you put in. Or how busy you are.

We've all seen people who stay busy — who even work hard — without adding any real value. They make the mistake of thinking effort should earn them a paycheck. You can respect them for trying, but you can't justify the cost of keeping them on board. Their careers are built on make-believe.

You'll be better off if you think in terms of being paid for performance — for the value you add — rather than for your tenure, good intentions, or activity level.

Prove your worth to the organization. Make a difference. Add enough value so everyone can see that something very important would be missing if you left.

- Pritchett and Associates

# 11

# Recommended Education and Training

*"The only thing worse than training your employees and losing them is not training them and keeping them."*

Zig Ziglar

In the nation's top B schools, including the University of Pennsylvania (Wharton), Northwestern, University of Chicago, Stanford, Harvard, and Michigan, more emphasis is now being placed on teamwork and leadership, and education is becoming more pragmatic and less theoretical. Wharton recently received very high marks because its MBA program emphasizes "people skills" and real world problems. Graduates from these schools are earning $100,000+/year and there is great demand for them.

## BETTER UNDERSTANDING YOURSELF AND OTHERS

Many companies are sending their executives and promising, future executives to The Center for Creative Leadership for leadership training. This six-day Leadership Development Program, offered in Greensboro, NC and several other sites across the country, is the hottest program in the country and its goal is to transform students into creative leaders, and not mere functional managers. The program's current cost is $4900. The program's underlying philosophy is that leadership is something which resides in nearly everyone as a potential, and by better understanding yourself, you can improve your way of leading.

Alumni of this program, myself included, say that the program helped boost self-confidence, helped put more balance in their lives, and taught them to be more effective at work and at home. Since 1974, nearly 40,000 managers from all over the world have subjected themselves to six days of psychological testing, lectures, and group exercises, under the watchful eyes of clinical psychologists, who provided continuous feedback. Fellow students also anonymously observed each other, delivering peer feedback on "feedback" day. These feedback sessions are often humbling experiences.

> Success is the peace of mind, which is a direct result of self-satisfaction in knowing that you did your best to become the best that you are capable of becoming using the abilities you have.
>
> - John R. Wooden

In my particular case, I found that the group exercises were particularly valuable to me. Being a strong extrovert, I often became frustrated over the limited participation of introverts in my class, and most of my class happened to be introverts. With the feedback I received, I was able to learn how to involve introverts, by asking them a lot of questions and giving them a lot of recognition and encouragement. My previous 24 management courses I took in undergraduate and graduate school hardly touched on the importance of getting everyone involved and how to encourage involvement. As a result, I overlooked introverts.

> Once you say, "I'm a professional," you commit yourself to a life-time of self-improvement.

Since 1986, I proactively seek out introverts to participate, no matter where they are hiding. It's an extrovert's job.

Today's leadership challenges require all of us to be *interdependent* on others. As individuals, we can't possibly be everything to everybody. In order to maximize our effectiveness, I believe that it is important to understand a great deal more about ourselves and our employees. There are several tools at our disposal and each can help us understand the dynamics of personality and how individuals respond differently to the same set of stimuli. More decisions in the future will be made by involving teams who will obtain information from many others.

Earlier in this book, we discussed how effective leaders use growth motivation. Change a leader and see what happens to productivity and morale. *It can go up or down.* A leader is a leader only if others are willing to follow, and many times we find that the person in a job is not well suited for it. If we knew more about the person, what motivates them, and who could motivate them, we could make changes that would benefit them and the company. We can adapt jobs to fit people and help people into jobs that better suit them, but it's very difficult to change people to fit jobs.

> The education of a man (or woman) is never completed until he (she) dies.
>
> - Robert E. Lee

In order to do this, we should know their personality type and value and understand the differences in each other. The Meyers-Briggs Type Indicator is one of several instruments which can be used to determine personality types. I have used the MBTI, as it often is called, and three others [the MFS (Managing for Success) personal profile system, Carlson Learning Systems Personal Survey System (DISC), and Advanced Interpersonal Skill Development System] successfully with my management employees (see chart at the end of this chapter).

Awareness of one's personality style and type and how we are perceived by others allows leaders to tailor their leadership style to the personalities of those employees working for them. Whether we like it or not, our employees can make or break us as effective leaders, and understanding them allows us to appeal to their strengths. Knowledge of one's employees (and each other) is invaluable and can be a big productivity booster in the organization.

> The only magic works is by hard work. But hard work can be fun.
>
> - Jim Henson

Another important quality I was able to reinforce by taking this program is my ability to make others feel important by constantly looking for the gold in them. Group exercises taught us how to say nice things to others. Since I finished the program in 1986, showing appreciation has become one of my trademarks.

---
Improvement begins with "I."
---

## WHERE TO GO FOR TRAINING

My recommendations regarding "ongoing" leadership training for your managers and aspiring managers would include:

- Sending one or more of your most promising managers to The Center for Creative Leadership Program.
- Have all management/supervision read selected books and/or listen to audio tapes on leadership and motivation once a month (especially those listed here).
- Encourage them to become a member of Toastmasters' International or take a Dale Carnegie course in public speaking.
- Once a quarter, show selected video tapes including Les Brown, Brian Tracy, Zig Ziglar, and Rich "MR POS" Wilkins, to graduates of "Strategies for Success" as a reinforcement to their learning.
- Once or twice a year, encourage your management team to attend a regional/national conference to keep up with technological advances.
- Bring in selected trainers on mentoring, team-building, and assessment training (personality profiles), such as Francie Dalton of Dalton Alliances.
- Hold regularly scheduled, open forums with all employees.
- Hold excellence workshops with all managers/supervisors quarterly to discuss how everything is progressing.
- Communicate, communicate, communicate with everyone in your sphere of influence.
- Personally mentor those who become actively involved in the process and are continuous learners.

## Lesson in Leadership

Investing in education and training to build effective leaders pays off. My own three-year research project, which resulted in my writing the book *Looking for the Gold*, proved to me that investing in employees is well worth the time, effort, and expense. Even in the most challenging environment of all — government — employees can be productive. A return on investment of over 100:1 was the bottom line.

Yes, it makes sense to invest in more training opportunities for employees. Don't you agree?

Your future begins now. Today is the turning point in your life. Follow my advice and make that little bit of extra effort to improve your people skills. You'll be glad you did.

Use the following chart to quickly determine your own personality style, as well as that of your boss, your peers, and your subordinates. The styles and identifiers will allow you to determine which ones are applicable. The remaining categories will give you information about their needs, the way they make decisions, the way they respond/react to feedback, and most importantly, how best to interact with them.

## Advanced Interpersonal Skills

| Style | Identifiers | Strongest Need | Decision Method | Reaction to Feedback | Secrets for Optimum Interaction |
|---|---|---|---|---|---|
| Commander | Abrupt, aloof, cold, poor delegators, confident, assertive, sense of urgency, solid eye contact, domineering, structured perfectionists | Control | Do it my way now! | Turn the tables<br><br>Attack | Be organized, clear and concise; listen; show how your idea will create order, increase control and enhance results, be direct, bottom line first, offer alternatives; negotiate, value their ability to implement |
| Attacker | Hostile, angry, grouchy, argumentative, demoralizing, intimidating, nasty, seek fault in others | Respect | Nasty<br><br>Just do it! | Interpret as personal abuse<br><br>Attack | Don't take it personally; show respect, be consistently responsive — not reactive, stick to the facts, prepare for lots of questions, value their ability to find loopholes |
| Avoider | Reserved, cautious, quiet, poor eye contact, superficial conversation, believe paying attention to something makes it worse, fear of risk, no initiative | Security | Delay<br><br>Use committees | Silence<br><br>Faces register nothing<br><br>Departure | Show how your idea will insulate and protect, make them feel safe; be calm, relate new to known, don't expect decisiveness or initiative, value their ability to follow instructions |

| | | | | |
|---|---|---|---|---|
| Drifter | Free spirited, easy going, disorganized, impulsive, chaotic, confusing, seem distant, ambiguous, change subject frequently, no follow-up, no closure, imaginative, improvisers, hate rules, hate facts, hate structure | Freedom | Who cares? | Change subject<br><br>Won't listen<br><br>Become distracted | Focus on fun; provide incentives, don't pressure or constrain, be casual, indirect and relaxed, give short compact assignments, provide variety, value their creativity and innovation |
| Pleaser | Nice, kind, agreeable, reassuring, sympathetic, give in easily, all others come first, need all to agree, hate conflict, won't confront problems, phobia re: anger | To be loved, accepted | How to do "X" and still retain your regard | Act hurt and cry<br><br>Pretend to agree | Take a personal interest in them, show how your idea will help and please all, provide references and guarantees; reassure, spend time with the pleaser's associates who will be affected by your idea, value their people skills |
| Performer | Flashy, loud, jovial, status conscious, fun to be with, show offs, take limelight, talkative, self-promoters, in a hurry, overcommitted | Recognition | Sell, sell, sell<br><br>Whatever will make self a star | Blame others<br><br>Deny fault<br><br>Rationalize | Make the performer a star, focus on concept, not details, clarify facts, use storytelling; entertain, stroke ego, value their sales/presentation skills |

## Advanced Interpersonal Skills (continued)

| Style | Identifiers | Strongest Need | Decision Method | Reaction to Feedback | Secrets for Optimum Interaction |
|---|---|---|---|---|---|
| Analytical | Precise, diligent, detailed, poor eye contact, monotone, focused on process — how and why, not innovative, overanalyze everything | Certainty | Avoidance<br><br>Reanalyze | Ask for examples and details<br><br>They then tell you their reasons | Be factual and provide technical content, provide written process with all details, give time to "think it over," be specific; show respect for detail, be prepared to answer all questions, show how each fact builds on another, value their analytical abilities |
| Achiever | Peaceful, happy, serene, self-directed and self-fulfilled, enjoys self and others, high self-esteem, interested in others, honest, effective | Competency | Driven by effectiveness and based on research | Thank you!<br><br>Tell me more!<br><br>They own their behavior | Be yourself! They will adapt to you |

- Courtesy of Dalton Alliances

# SUCCESS STORIES

## If I Had My Life to Live Over

If I had my life to live over, I'd dare to make more mistakes next time. I'd relax, I'd limber up. I would be sillier than I've been this trip. I would take fewer things seriously, take more chances, take more trips. I'd climb more mountains, and swim more rivers. I would eat more ice cream and less beans. I would, perhaps, have more actual troubles, but I'd have fewer imaginary ones. You see, I'm one of those people who lived seriously, sanely, hour after hour, day after day. Oh, I've had my moments, and if I had it to do over again, I'd have more of them. I've been one of those persons who never goes anywhere without a thermometer, a hot-water bottle, a raincoat, and a parachute. If I had my life to live over, I would start going barefoot earlier in the spring, and stay that way later in the fall. I would go to more dances, I would ride more merry-go-rounds. I would pick more daisies.

*- The Speaker's Sourcebook*

## Anecdotes About Confidence

The next time you're bombarded with criticism, remember Colonel George Washington Goethals, the man who successfully completed the Panama Canal. He had problems enough with the geography and climate involved, yet he still had to endure the carping criticism of many busybodies back home who kept predicting that he would never complete this project. But he steadfastly stuck to the task and said nothing. "Aren't you going to answer these critics?" an associate asked. "In time," Goethals replied. "How?" "With the canal," Goethals said.

*- The Speaker's Sourcebook*

## Don't Let Others Stop You

Others can stop you temporarily, but you are the only one who can do it permanently.

Consider this: An elephant can easily pick up a one-ton load with its trunk. How is it then that, at the circus, these huge creatures stand quietly tied to a small wooden stake?

While the elephant is still young and not so strong, it is tied by a heavy chain to an immovable iron stake. It tries to break the chain but soon discovers that no matter how hard it tries, it cannot break loose. As the elephant grows and becomes strong, it never again tries to break loose because it thinks it cannot.

**Many intelligent adults behave like the circus elephant. They remain restrained in thought and action all their lives. They never move further than the boundaries of their self-imposed limitation.**

*- The Speaker's Sourcebook*

## Become Your Best

The poet Robert Browning said, "My business is not to remake myself, but to make the absolute best of what God made."

Art Linkletter has an excellent philosophy for making your best better:

Do a little more than you're paid to;
Give a little more than you have to;
Try a little harder than you want to;
Aim a little higher than you think possible;
And give a lot of thanks to God for health, family, and friends.

*- The Working Communicator*

# Epilogue

*"We should live our lives as though Christ was coming this afternoon."*

Jimmy Carter

Well, what do you think? Was the journey worth it? My objective was to encourage you to become the type of leader you were destined to be and then influence others, by example, to follow in your footsteps.

Will it be easy? No, it won't; but it is achievable and you CAN do it. Don't EVER give up trying. As Dr. Robert Schuler has said, "failure only occurs when you stop trying."

I do hope that you'll refer to this book time and again for reinforcement along the way and use the additional resources which follow. And you can call me personally, if you'd like.

Sincerely,

*Al Migs Damiani*

A. S. Migs Damiani

# Resources for Your Personal/Professional Growth

## SUGGESTED BOOKS:

*The Speaker's Sourcebook* by Glenn Van Ekeren
*Flight of the Buffalo* by James A. Belasco and Ralph C. Stayer
*How to Win Friends and Influence People* by Dale Carnegie
*The 7 Habits of Highly Effective People* by Stephen Covey
*Principle Centered Leadership* by Stephen Covey
*Mining Group Gold* by Thomas Kayser
*If It Ain't Broke... Break It* by Robert Kriegal
*The Art of Self-Leadership* by Charles C. Manz
*Corporate Coach* by James B. Miller
*This Incredible Century* by Norman Vincent Peale
*Team Reconstruction — Building A High Performance Work Group During Change* by Price Pritchett and Ron Pound
*The Healthy Company* by Robert H. Rosen, Ph.D. with Lisa Berger
*Leading People* by Robert H. Rosen, Ph.D.
*The Team Handbook* by Peter Scholtes
*Commit to Quality* by Patrick Townsend
*Further Up the Organization* by Robert Townsend
*Powerful Stuff* by Rich "MR POS" Wilkins
*Building A POSitive Attitude* by Rich "MR POS" Wilkins

*Going Beyond a Positive Mental Attitude* by Rich "MR POS"
Wilkins
*See You At The Top* by Zig Ziglar
*Over The Top* by Zig Ziglar
*Looking For The Gold* by A.S. Migs Damiani

## VIDEO TRAINING TAPES:

"You Deserve" by Les Brown
"It's Possible" by Les Brown
"The Power of Change" by Les Brown
"The Courage to Live Your Dreams" by Les Brown
"Seven Habits of Highly Effective People" by Stephen R. Covey
"The Chameleon's Edge" by Francie Dalton
"The Leadership Alliance" by Tom Peters
"Excellence in the Public Sector" by Tom Peters
"Success Secrets of Self Made Millionaires" by Brian Tracy
"The Effective Manager" (Motivating People Toward Peak
Performance) by Brian Tracy
"Building A Positive Attitude Toward Yourself and Others" by
Rich "MR POS" Wilkins
"Empowering Positive Attitudes" by Rich "MR POS" Wilkins
"Raising Positive Kids in a Negative World" (1 tape) by Zig
Ziglar
"Changing the Picture" by Zig Ziglar
"Strategies for Success" (6 tapes) by Zig Ziglar
"Goals" (1 tape) by Zig Ziglar
"How To Be A Winner" (1 tape) by Zig Ziglar
"5 Steps to Selling" (1 tape) by Zig Ziglar
"Courtship After Marriage" (1 tape) by Zig Ziglar

## AUDIO TRAINING TAPES:

"How to Win Friends and Influence People" (8 tapes) by Dale
Carnegie
"The New Masters of Excellence" (6 tapes) by Tom Peters

"Thriving on Chaos" (6 tapes) by Tom Peters
"The Psychology of Achievement" (6 tapes) by Brian Tracy
"Success Secrets of Self Made Millionaires" by Brian Tracy
"Seeing John Brown Through John Brown's Eyes" (6 tapes) by
    Rich "MR POS" Wilkins
"How to Be A Winner" (1 tape) by Zig Ziglar
"Secrets of Closing the Sale" (12 tapes) by Zig Ziglar
"How to Stay Motivated" (18 tapes) by Zig Ziglar

## FOR FURTHER INFORMATION, CONTACT:

Rich Wilkins & Co.
Rich "MR POS" Wilkins     1-800-944-7269
Zig Ziglar Corporation     1-800-527-0306
                      (972) 991-1853 (fax)
A.S. Migs Damiani       (202) 333-4977
                      (202) 342-5199 (fax)
                      migsd@donohoe.com (e-mail)
Dalton Alliances         1-800-442-3603
Francie Dalton           (410) 360-2100
                      (410) 360-4442 (fax)

# Words of Inspiration

Self-esteem is the key to improving employee achievement and responsibility.

Common sense is not so common.
- *Voltaire*

Imagination is more important than knowledge.
- *Albert Einstein*

All our dreams can come true — if we have the courage to pursue them.
- *Walt Disney*

If a person has done his best, what else is there?
- *George S. Patton*

Ninety percent of what you are is what you think you are.
- *Ted Turner*

A friend is a present you give yourself.
- *Robert Louis Stevenson*

Our greatest glory is not in never falling, but in rising every time we fall.
- *Confucius*

Whether you think you can or think you can't — you are right.
- *Henry Ford*

Nothing great was ever achieved without enthusiasm.
- *Ralph Waldo Emerson*

We need to fill a child's bucket of self esteem so high that the rest of the world can't poke enough holes in it to drain it dry.

Every job is a self-portrait of the person who did it. Autograph your work with excellence!

Never tell people how to do things. Tell them what to do and they will surprise you with their ingenuity.

3 R's of management — recognize, reward, reinforce (encourage).

A measure of a person's greatness is his/her goodness.
- *Benjamin Franklin*

If you cannot accept losing, you cannot win.
- *Vince Lombardi*

We must be dream makers and create realities out of our dreams and dreams out of our realities.
- *Willy Wonka*

When we give 100% we compete; 110% we succeed.

Take the "I will" over the IQ every time.

I have offended God and mankind because my work didn't reach the quality it should have.
- *Leonardo da Vinci*

Accomplishment will prove to be a journey, not a destination.
- *Dwight D. Eisenhower*

We must change to master change.
- *Lyndon Johnson*

People forget how fast you did a job — but they remember how well you did it.
- *Howard Newton*

Striving for excellence motivates you; striving for perfection is demoralizing.
- *Harriet Braiker*

Success is getting up just one more time than you fall down.
- *Doc Blakely*

Reach down and help others up. If we don't, we will eventually be pulled down.
- *Zig Ziglar*

It's not your aptitude, but your attitude that will determine your altitude.
- *Zig Ziglar*

Ability without honor has no value.
- *Zig Ziglar*

You are what you are and where you are because of what goes into your mind.
- *Zig Ziglar*

Success in life is not so much a matter of talent or opportunity as it is of concentration and perseverance.

The surest way not to fail is to determine to succeed.

If I miss one day's practice, I notice it. If I miss two days, the critics notice it. If I miss three days, the audience notices it.
- *Ignace Paderewski*

The greatest pleasure in life is doing what people say can't be done.

If you want to give a man credit, do it in writing. If you want to give him hell, do it over the phone.
- *Lee Iacocca*

Bravery is the capacity to perform properly even when scared half to death.
- *General Omar Bradley*

A pint of sweat will save a gallon of blood.
- *General George S. Patton*

God gives every bird its food, but he does not throw it into the nest.
- *J.G .Holland*

A poor surgeon hurts one person at a time. A poor teacher hurts 30.
- *Ernest Boyer*

A dwarf standing on the shoulders of a giant may see further than a giant himself.
- *Robert Burton*

You can't plant a seed and pick the fruit the next morning.
- *Jesse Jackson*

You have to love your children unselfishly. That's hard, but it's the only way.
- *Barbara Bush*

Whoever is happy will make others happy too.
- *Anne Frank*

It's never too late to be what you might have been.
- *George Eliot*

Do your work with your whole heart and you will succeed — there's so little competition.
- *Elbert Hubbard*

If you stop growing today, you stop teaching tomorrow.

In the end, it is important to remember that we cannot become what we need to be by remaining what we are.
- *Max DePree*

Positive attitudes, create positive people, creating a positive world.
- *Raphael Hu*

Do you want a raise — ask for more work.

Never, never quit. Never, never, never, never quit.
- *Winston Churchill*

Success starts with serving others.
- *Zig Ziglar*

A successful life starts with a successful day.
- *Zig Ziglar*

Most locked doors are in your mind.

Go as far as you can see and when you get there, you'll be able to see further.
- *Zig Ziglar*

If you wait around for others to become lovable before you love them, the wait will be endless.

Our attitude toward other people influences greatly what they will become.

What people need more than anything else is encouragement.
- *Andrew Greeley*

Recognize that Talent is spelled W-O-R-K.
- *Robert Schuller*

Only read novels. For the only thing that matters in business is personal relationships.
- *Tom Peters*

I don't have to work with people I don't like.
- *Warren Buffett*

This is what it's all about: if you can't have fun at it, there's no sense hanging around.
- *Joe Montana*

Hell, there are no rules here — we're trying to accomplish something.
- *Thomas A. Edison*

To decide not to decide is a decision. To fail to decide is a failure.
- *George S. Patton*

We should not let fear hold us back from our hopes.
- *John F. Kennedy*

Fear of failure. That's the thrill. It's what gets your heart rate up.
- *Jim Barksdale*

Change your thoughts and you change your world.
- *Norman Vincent Peale*

To risk creates the possibility of failure ... not to risk insures it.

*The Employees' ROI*
  R  –  RESPECTS
  O  –  IS OPEN
  I  –  INFORMS

Your best friend is that person who brings the best out of you.
- *Henry Ford*

I believe we are here for a reason.
I believe that as each day unfolds,
We see less of the shadow
and more of the sun,
less of the tarnish
and more of the gold.
- *C. Hawkinson*

We make a living by what we get. We make a life by what we give.
- *Winston Churchill*

An investment in knowledge pays the best interest.
- *Benjamin Franklin*

Your children need your presence more than your presents.
- *Jesse Jackson*

Quality is not only making sure our customers are happy, but making sure our employees are happy.

Our character is what we do when we think no one is looking.

People are the most important ingredient in a company and we always forget it. It is not systems, not computers.
- *Chuck Lauer*

Stop whining and start winning.

People don't care how much you know until they know how much you care. You demonstrate caring by helping people accomplish their objectives.
- *Cavett Robert*

There is no failure except in no longer trying.
- *Elbert Hubbard*

Change is the law of life, and those who look only to the past or present are certain to miss the future.
- *John F. Kennedy*

**I** fear there will be no future for those who do not change.
- *Louis L'Amour*

**If** you keep on doing what you've been doing, you're going to keep on getting what you've been getting.
- *Zig Ziglar*

**C** – COMMUNICATES
**A** – APPRECIATES
**R** – RECOGNIZES, REWARDS
**E** – ENCOURAGES
**S** – SHARES

**D**o things *Exactly Right* the first time! It's the only time you get paid for it!

**W**hen we become "other-people" centered, we will receive the true rewards of life.
- *Zig Ziglar*

**W**hen we do things for ourselves we take them to our grave. When we do things for others we leave them behind.

**A**lways forgive your enemies — nothing annoys them so much.
- *Oscar Wilde*

**I**nsanity is doing the same thing over and over again, expecting different results.
- *Rita Mae Brown*

**B**ureaucracy is nothing more than a hardening of an organization's arteries.
- *Managing Incompetence by William J. Anthony*

**T**he most pernicious myth of all is that leadership is reserved for only a few of us.
- *James N. Kouzes and Barry Z. Posner*

There are no great people, just ordinary people who set different goals.
- *Robert Schuller*

Desire creates the power.
- *Raymond Holliwell*

In the middle of difficulty lies opportunity.
- *Albert Einstein*

Look at people; recognize them, accept them as they are, without wanting to change them.
- *Helen Beginton*

Write a thank you note to all the supervisors of someone who has helped you, thanking them for having such a terrific employee.

More people would learn from their mistakes if they weren't so busy denying that they made them.

You know you're #1 when: you *love* what you do.

While self-preservation is one of the first instructs of nature, consideration for others is the keystone of civilization.
- *Walt Disney*

Being able to adapt to change is the key to success and happiness.
- *Lee Iacocca*

When you have the power to change things and you don't, that is a failure of leadership.
- *Lee Iacocca*

When you help someone over the hill, you're that much nearer the top yourself.

The one thing worse than a quitter is the one who is afraid to begin.

Minds are like parachutes — they only function when open.

Failure is not defeat — until you stop trying.

Do what you can with what you have where you are.
- *Teddy Roosevelt*

Funny how a dollar looks so big when you take it to church and so small when you take it to the store.
- *Frank Clark*

The way to learn is to begin.

All the wonders you seek are within yourself.
- *Sir Thomas Brown*

Everyone thinks of changing humanity and nobody thinks of changing himself.

Patience is the ability to put up with people you'd like to put down.

A little smile adds a great deal to your face value.

Years wrinkle the skin, but lack of enthusiasm wrinkles the soul.
- *Norman Vincent Peale*

There is no thrill like doing something you didn't know you could.
- *Marjorie Holmes*

If you are willing to admit when you are wrong, you are right.

Example is not the main way in influencing others. It is the only thing.
- *Albert Schweitzer*

I can alter my life by altering the attitude of my mind.

Always do right. This will gratify some people and astonish the rest.
- *Mark Twain*

Children are like wet cement. Whatever falls on them makes an impression.
- *Haim Ginott*

Friendship is the only cement that can hold the world together.

Be a living expression of God's kindness.
- *Mother Teresa*

Do not follow where the path leads. Go where there is no path and leave a trail.

Your dreams come true when you act to turn them into realities.

Some people give and forgive; others get and forget.

The control center of your life is your attitude.

People who like others are people others like.

Make one person happy each day, even if it's yourself.

Our chief want is someone who will inspire us to be what we know we could be.
- *Ralph Waldo Emerson*

Setting an example is not the main means of influencing another; it is the only means.
- *Albert Einstein*

They conquer who believe they can.
- *Ralph Waldo Emerson*

The deepest urge in human nature is the desire to be important.
- *John Dewey*

Success or failure is caused more by mental attitude than by mental capacity.
- *Sir Walter Scott*

Within you lies a power greater than what lies before you.

The most important advice I could give an executive: seek every opportunity to give a speech.
- *Robert E. Mercer*

Vision is the art of seeing the invisible.
- *Jonathan Swift*

The only people who never fail are those who never try.
- *Ilka Chase*

Don't find fault, find a remedy.

No one can become rich without enriching others.
- *Andrew Carnegie*

The sweetest of all sounds is praise.

All things come to him who goes after them.

Being number one is easier than remaining number one.
- *Bill Bradley, U.S. Senate*

Everyone needs to feel like somebody.

Handle your anger by preventing its buildup.
- *Dave Galloway*

It's not who is right but what is right.

I always view problems as opportunities in work clothes.
- *Henry J. Kaiser*

You learn from successful failures.

A sincere compliment is one of the most effective tools to teach and motivate others.

You have within you all of the qualities necessary for success.

You get the best out of others when you give the best of yourself.
- *Harvey Firestone*

You do not lead by hitting people over the head - that's assault, not leadership.
- *Dwight D. Eisenhower*

An army of deer led by a lion is more to be feared than an army of lions led by a deer.

Strange as it may sound, great leaders gain authority by giving it away.

Most business failures don't stem from bad times. They come from poor management, and the bad times just precipitate the crisis.
- *Thomas P. Murphy*

Confidence is contagious. So is lack of confidence.
- *Orson Wells*

Before you can score, you must first have a goal.

You must manage as if you need your employees more than they need you.
- *Peter Drucker*

The horse never knows I'm there until he needs me.
- *Willie Shoemaker*

For every criticism you make, make sure that you give the person four compliments.

Your face says it all.
- *Abraham Lincoln*

Success is 99% failure.
- *Soichiro Honda*

Good enough never is.
- *Debbie Fields*

If you want the rainbow, you gotta put up with the rain.
- *Dolly Parton*

It is what we do easily and what we like to do that we do well.
- *Orison Swett Marden*

Delay is preferable to error.
- *Thomas Jefferson*

Writing forces you to THINK more deeply.
- *Christopher Thaiss*

Them that's going, get on the wagon. Them that ain't, get out of the way.
- *A Georgia Preacher*

What this country needs is dirtier fingernails and cleaner minds.
- *Will Rogers*

Managers learn while they teach.

The more workers feel needed, the more likely they are to be there, and on time.

Man is great only when he is kneeling.
- *Pope Pius XII*

Find the job you love and you will never have to work a day in your life.
- *Jim Fox*

Learn how to pay compliments and start at home.
- *Letitia Baldrage*

It is better to have one person working with you than having three people working for you.
- *Dwight D. Eisenhower*

The way to develop the best that is in a person is by appreciation and encouragement.
- *Charles Schwab*

I have had a great many troubles, but most of them never happen.
- *Mark Twain*

Next to God, we are indebted to women; first for life itself, and then for making it worth having.
- *Bovee*

You miss 100% of the shots you don't take.
- *Wayne Gretzky*

People ask for criticism but they want praise.

You may be disappointed if you fail, but you are doomed if you don't try.
- *Beverly Sills*

Most people quit looking for work as soon as they find a job.
- *Zig Ziglar*

If you refuse to accept anything but the best, you often get it.
- *W. Somerset Maugham*

I'd rather be a failure at something I enjoy than be a success at something I hate.
- *George Burns*

There are no shortcuts to any place worth going.
- *Beverly Sills*

Children have more need of models than of critics.
- *Carolyn Coats*

A friend is a lot of things, but a critic he isn't.
- *Bern Williams*

Winners never quit and quitters never win.
- *Vince Lombardi*

If dandelions were hard to grow, they would be most welcome on any lawn.
- *Andrew Mason*

I always prefer to believe the best of everybody.
- *Rudyard Kipling*

You must do the things you think you cannot do.
- *Eleanor Roosevelt*

Eighty percent of success is showing up.
- *Woody Allen*

Success is turning knowledge into positive action.
- *Dorothy Leeds*

The greatest leaders throughout history have been notoriously poor followers.
- *Katheryn Collins*

You can't shake hands with a clenched fist.
- *Indira Gandhi*

She's the kind of woman who climbed the ladder of success — wrong by wrong.
- *Mae West*

# Notes

# Notes

# Notes

# Notes

# Notes

# Notes

# Notes

# Notes

# Notes